IN THE
EVENING,
WE'LL
DANCE

TEXT COPYRIGHT © 2025 BY ANNE-MARIE ERICKSON.
All rights reserved. No part of this book may be reproduced without permission of the Author and Publisher.
Cover and text design by Anton Khodakovsky.
Cover photograph by John Connelly; author photograph by Janna Salmela.
All interior photographs by Anne-Marie Erickson, except for The Sun Newspapers photograph of Dick Cain (photographer unknown), the eclipse image by Adam McCoid, and the log house photograph by Dick Cain.
Excerpts from the essay "I'm My Own Person" have been published in *Perspectives on Social and Material Fractures in Care*. Ed. Colleen R. Greer and Debra F. Peterson. Hershey, PA: IGI Global, 2024.

Printed and bound in the United States.
First printing, Summer, 2025
10 9 8 7 6 5 4 3 2 1

Library of Congress Cataloging Number: 2024028855
ISBN 978-1666406955 (paperback)
ISBN 978-1666406962 (eBook)

Holy Cow! Press projects are funded in part by grant awards from the Ben and Jeanne Overman Charitable Trust, the Elmer L. and Eleanor J. Andersen Foundation, The Lenfestey Family Foundation, The Woessner Freeman Family Foundation, and by gifts from generous individual donors. We are grateful to Springboard for the Arts for their support as our fiscal sponsor.

Holy Cow! Press books are distributed to the trade by Consortium Book Sales & Distribution, c/o Ingram Publisher Services, Inc., 210 American Drive, Jackson, TN 38301.

For inquiries, please write to: Holy Cow! Press, Post Office Box 3170, Mount Royal Station, Duluth, MN 55803.

Visit www.holycowpress.org

IN THE EVENING, WE'LL DANCE

A Memoir in Essays on Love & Dementia

Anne-Marie Erickson

Holy Cow! Press
Duluth, Minnesota
2025

In memory & in honor of
Dick Cain
April 26, 1932-October 30, 2015
Then, Now, Always

For
Susan Hawkinson,
*who urged me to begin this book
& continued to believe in it*

Contents

Prologue	1
PART 1. SEEKING, LOVING, MARRYING	**5**
Chapter 1. The Two of Us Have Been Asked to Say Something Wonderful	7
Chapter 2. When I Was a Young Man Courting the Girls	13
Chapter 3. Wally and Ruth Are in Mexico	17
Chapter 4. Are We Married?	19
Chapter 5. Kiss, Kiss	25
Chapter 6. We Built It	33
Chapter 7. I Still See in the Eyes of My Wife. Beautiful!	37
PART 2. LOSING, RE-COLLECTING	**47**
Chapter 8. I'm Making More Mistakes	49
Chapter 9. I'm My Own Person	63
Chapter 10. Jenny, Anna, Joe	79
Chapter 11. Yesterday I Knew Who That Was	87
PART 3. BATTERED, NOT BROKEN	**93**
Chapter 12. Who Are You?	95
Chapter 13. That's Not Becoming of You	103
Chapter 14. Annie, Can We Be Done with This Now?	113
Chapter 15. I Can't Avoid Moving on to the Horror	117
Chapter 16. I Was Overpowered	135
Chapter 17. What Is, Is	139
PART 4. SUSTAINING, UNSELFING, GROWING	**145**
Chapter 18. I Appreciate You Doing This	147
Chapter 19. There's So Much to Say, but I'm Not Capable	153
Chapter 20. Don't Forget the Singing	161
Chapter 21. This Crown Is Heavy	169
Chapter 22. Pursue Spiritual Growth	181

PART 5. LEAVE-TAKING **185**

    Chapter 23. You Are Me   187

    Chapter 24. In the Evening, We'll Dance   197

Epilogue   211

For Further Reading   215

Acknowledgments   219

About the Author   221

| Prologue

I often dream of my late husband. Sometimes he's healthy. Sometimes he's ill with dementia. Sometimes he's dead.

≈

One year after his death, I had this dream: *I stand naked in a room. It's raining. Wind flings wet leaves against the large windows in the old brick building. Green, pale green, and blue leaves adhere to the wet glass. The muted sounds of wind and rain envelop me. Warmth radiates from my body. A man appears in a darkened room across the way, his back to me. I call out. I want to show myself to him.*

≈

In many ways, our story is one of wanting.

I was twenty-four, and I wanted to meet an older man—a man who knew who he was, what he stood for, and what he wanted. Who knew how to love.

I met a man who was forty-one. He was tall and sinewy, with the poise of an assured athlete. His kind eyes held me in a steady gaze.

I wanted him and he wanted me—*want*, in the sense of a strong attraction. *Want*, in the sense of desire. I wanted to listen to his sonorous voice, to drink it in. I wanted to drink him in and savor his otherness.

I had no desire to flirt or play games. I was heedless of propriety, and I was ardent. Wanton. I ran my hand up his long, muscled thigh, then kissed him. I got what I wanted.

≈

I didn't want to be with a man who told me what I wanted to hear. I wanted candor. I came to understand that his integrity was what I most admired about Dick Cain.

I wanted to be by his side, to partner with him in parenting his three children, in our writing, and in our work. I wanted to sustain our dialogues and debates, to pursue questions and aspirations together. I wanted to divine what I was made of.

≈

We wanted to live deliberately. We wanted to be aware of the sun's station in the sky, season to season. We wanted to live our quotidian lives—scooping water, tending fire—with regard. So, five years after we met, we built a simple log cabin in Minnesota's North Woods.

And thus we lived for almost thirty years. We did not want for much. Then his memory began to wane, when he was sixty-six. I didn't want to see the signs. I didn't want to say, "My beloved has dementia." I wanted him back: the vivid, sexy, witty, quick, and curious man. But I could not will the disease away. I could not stay its incessant advance. For all my wanting, I could not, would not, be able to get him back as he had been.

≈

Dream: *I've lost him in a crowded room. I panic. "Dick, where are you?"*

≈

I wanted us to go about living our lives as best we could. We would remain, together, in our home for as long as we could. We'd live in the moment, attending art openings and concerts, enjoying walks, our gardens, and our friends. Sometimes, we'd simply sit in silence and watch lake waters ripple or the sun set.

Throughout that time, we leaned on the powers of love and language. When words began to fail him, he recast language in novel ways. I wanted to capture his coinages.

I wanted to make meaning of it all, so I recorded our passage through the seventeen years of his decline. I needed to shape sentences into some kind of order amid dementia's disorder. I wrote onto the silence of a blank page in the silence of the night, while he slept. I wove our story into essays.

I wanted to tell the story of our experience, as I understood it. I wanted to write an account of dementia as it manifested itself in the singularity of Dick Cain. I wanted to remain heedful of his dignity while bearing unflinching witness. I witnessed, but at times I couldn't be certain of what I was seeing. Due to the dementia, Dick often struggled to articulate what he felt or meant. I had to speculate: *I wonder. Perhaps. Possibly. Maybe.*

I wanted to be attentive to his observations, neologisms, notes, jokes, songs, and anguished cries. I entitled my essays with his words—words he spoke or wrote over the years of his decline.

≈

Dream: *One of his caregivers tells me that Dick has been writing minuets, but sometimes he doesn't get the sixteenth notes right.*

≈

I wanted to be with him, even late in his life, when he was toothless, stooped, his hair disheveled, beard unkempt. I told him he was my beautiful husband. And he was. Even as dementia altered him and the life we'd built together, I wanted to remain in the light of his love.

He held fast to language, to his integrity, and to life. He declared, "Life is beautiful." He said, "I love life as it is."

Then he grew frail and began to fail. He told me, "I've had enough of life." He wanted to take leave of this world.

≈

Dream: *Dick is living by a dark and dismal sea. Cold waves encroach on his rough, spare hut.*

≈

I did not want him to die. But he did.

I wanted him back, in order to make amends for the unraveling of my patience, for flare-ups fueled by fear. I wanted to reassure him that I survived, my *joie de vivre* unscathed. To say, once again, that our love abides.

After his death, I felt a profound longing, a deep want—*want* in the original meaning of the word, the Old Norse *vanta*, to be without. Uprooted, I hung in midair, hopelessly aching to be earthed in my husband again.

So I brought my beloved back into the world with these words.

PART 1

Seeking, Loving, Marrying

CHAPTER 1

The Two of Us Have Been Asked to Say Something Wonderful

In July of 2015, four months before he died of complications related to dementia, my husband said to me, "The two of us have been asked to say something wonderful." It seemed important, so I wrote it down.

The two of us

Not *I*. Not *you*. Not *we*. But *the two*, discrete yet coupled, as we'd always been. "Two solitudes," as Rilke puts it, who "protect and border and salute each other."

have been asked

I wish I'd inquired as to who he thought had asked us, but I doubt he'd have been able to reply. He was in the late stages of dementia.

"People need to hear your story," our friend Susan urged me more than a decade ago. "They're so afraid of dementia, yet you two live with so much love and joy." I surmised that we might *have been asked* by the people to whom Susan referred.

to say

To write is *to say*. The two of us had been writing partners for decades, reading and commenting on one another's work. However, for several years Dick had been unable to read or write because of his dementia—this man who had been a perceptive reader and an adept journalist and editor. Nevertheless, Dick clung to his identity as a writer. Just six months before his death, he said, "Hand. Finger. I still have time to write."

He usually was able to express his basic needs and declare his love for me, but, at times, his attempts at communication resembled a secret code. That intrigued me. So I became Dick's amanuensis, taking dictation. I hoped that by paying close attention to what he said, I could puzzle out what he was thinking and feeling.

I'd sit next to him, listening intently as he spoke. I'd inform him that I was taking notes. "You say some amazing things," I'd tell him. He seemed pleased. I also told Dick that I was writing essays about him. When I'd ask if he wanted to hear an excerpt, he always said, "Yes." I'd remind him, "This is about *you*!" He listened carefully, but, after a few minutes, he'd grow restive. He was lost, unable to track the sequence of sentences, the language pouring over him.

I chose to interpret Dick's declaration that we'd *been asked to say something wonderful* as his approval of my writing project, each essay inspired by his words.

something wonderful.

I asked him, "Wonderful? Such as?" but got no response. What might Dick have meant by this? He believed that our love was something wonderful, as did I. But I don't think that was the sole message.

It was near the end of his life, a life ravaged for seventeen years by dementia. How could so many losses over such a long period be *wonderful*? How could anything involving dementia possibly be *wonderful*? And yet, in many ways, it was full of wonder.

≈

This is the story of our search for meaning and for a way of being in the face of dementia. It's my testament to what remains and what was gained in the midst of loss.

Dementia shattered our life as we'd known it. It shattered any sense of certainty and control we might have had. Things often fell apart during the years of my husband's decline. But when something falls apart, you can see what it's made of. Living with Dick's dementia revealed insights into what our love, our marriage—what my husband and I—were made of.

The *something wonderful* is this story, our story. Dementia is not *the* story; it's only one part of the narrative. Our story is one of endurance—of self, of language, and of love. It is also a story of transcendence.

≈

Dick's efforts to communicate moved me; his neologisms fascinated me. Until the end, he would speak with correct syntax. Then he'd arrive at a gap, a word lost or hidden. He'd fling a series of word-like sounds across the chasm, like a makeshift bridge spanning a gorge. Sometimes, Dick would look back at the sentence he'd just traversed. He observed, "Quite a *niff*. No. Quite a *bit*. What the hell am I saying? I said '*Niff.*' That's a new word!"

While I dashed around his room swatting at a fly, he said, "All you do is go around hitting *pankyppers*." I typed this delightful coinage into my phone; autocorrect replaced it with *pan kippers*. It converted *swidget* into *swishers*. *Phoreves*, which he spoke and then spelled out, became *phone essays*. Frustrated, I'd backtrack, correcting the correction. He might well have felt a similar vexation; the real word resided somewhere in his mind, but he couldn't locate it.

I have hundreds of such entries on my phone. For more than nine years, beginning in 2006, I'd made notes whenever Dick said something striking, funny, or wise. Like coins spilled from a worn pouch, I hoarded his words.

I'd scribble down what he'd said during dinner parties, in restaurants, at clinics. I made notes in my commonplace book, engagement calendar, on scraps of paper, index cards, napkins, playbills—whatever was at hand. They're stuffed into document boxes, taped into journals, stashed in computer files.

The notes are mementos, reminders of who he was, who we were. When I'd misplace one, I'd grow frantic as I searched. I realized that this might well have been how he felt when memories—and then words—failed him.

9

≈

The disappearance of a beloved happens in many ways, for many reasons. People change. Grow remote. Divorce. Move away. Lose touch. Get ill. Die.

In our case, we held on to a long love in the face of loss upon loss. He had dementia, but he didn't disappear. Neither did I. We continued to see and to know and to love one another.

"I'm terrified of losing you in me," Francisco Goldman writes of the loss of his wife, Aura Estrada, in his autobiographical novel, *Say Her Name*. The reviewer Robin Romm observes that Goldman "furiously attempts to hold on to what can be kept: mittens, hats, rings, as if they have the power to anchor him in the world."

Like Goldman, I want to hang on to what can be preserved: my husband's watch, a favorite sweater, photographs, his letters and notes. It's a way of keeping both me and my memories of him anchored in the world. Through writing, I slowly sort through, piece together, and make sense of our lived experience. My efforts often are illuminated by my husband's own words. Even in death, Dick Cain remains my writing partner.

I write to honor the memory of my late husband. *Memory* is related to the Old English word *murnan*, meaning "to mourn."

≈

Some people would tell me that I was a "saint" for staying by my husband's side those many years. Why did they want to elevate me? Perhaps because my situation stirred up their fears and spurred self-scrutiny: *Would I be as strong? Would I be as steadfast?*

The answers are unique to each person and situation. It would depend on how the dementia might manifest itself in a loved one. It would depend on their relationship to one another, their needs, their conceptions of burden and of commitment. They'd have to make their own decisions, as I'd made mine.

I'm no saint. I'm flawed, riddled with failings, fears, guilts, and doubts. I did not embrace the role of caregiver. I want to be clear about this: I have no need to be needed. That's why I elected not to have any babies; I balked at their utter dependence. I couldn't have foreseen that my independent husband would become utterly dependent on me someday.

As he declined, tangles of memories—dates, names, places—snarled in his mind. He grew frustrated as he attempted to unravel them. The disease sapped his physical abilities, too, slowly consuming what had been a wiry, agile body. Eventually, he could no longer walk.

Like me, Dick probably felt so alone at times. Abandoned. On a few occasions—when I had to leave him at the hospital and, later, at an assisted living home—he yelled my name and kicked the door as it closed behind me.

I anchored him; as long as I was with him, he knew who he was. Actually, the word *anchorage* might be more fitting. An anchor is a weighty object; an anchorage is a place, a berth where a vessel can be harbored.

In a poem entitled "To the Harbormaster," Frank O'Hara writes, "To / you I offer my hull and the tattered cordage / of my will." To my husband, I offered my self: the flawed and mortal hull of my body and the worn ropes of my will.

He was the love of my life. I could not set him adrift.

CHAPTER 2

When I Was a Young Man Courting the Girls

For a long time in Dick's decline, he could still recite the opening lines from T.S. Eliot's "The Love Song of J. Alfred Prufrock": *Let us go then, you and I.* And the first lines of Dylan Thomas's poem "Lament": *When I was a windy boy and a bit / And the black spit of the chapel fold.*

He always omitted the third line, *Sighed the old ram rod, dying of women.* Was it a failure of memory or a deliberate avoidance? In his mid-seventies, Dick probably didn't want to think of himself as old. But what of the women? When he was married to his first wife, Dick occasionally had, as Thomas writes, *wooed / Whoever I would with my wicked eyes.*

Those eyes. They certainly could be seductive. Early in our relationship, I'd shot a black-and-white photo of Dick reclining on the sofa, a white kitten on his chest, his head of wavy, greying hair cushioned by the armrest, his dark eyes looking directly at me. I'd tacked it on my cubicle wall at work.

During breaks from the tedium of typing invoices, I'd glance at his likeness to remind myself why, in my mid-twenties, I'd become step-mother to his three teen-aged children. The picture had been up only a week or two when another billing clerk stopped by my desk. "I'd take down that photo if I were you," she said.

"Why?"

"It's too sexy."

She didn't need to elaborate. It was those seductive eyes, their long lashes, the arch of his eyebrows. Often, he'd raise his right brow slightly, which gave his face an air of curiosity or amusement—or, in the photo in question, a come-hither look.

≈

Not long before I met Dick, I'd dated a handsome man with the tanned face and chiseled features of the cowboys in those old Marlboro ads. I quickly wearied of such perfection. But I never tired of gazing at Dick's face, with its beguiling imperfections: the large Roman nose, offset by his wide-set eyes and strong brow; the sharp definition of his temples and cheekbones.

Some people told me that Dick looked distinguished. But I thought the unruly rumple of his hair and the raffish glint in his eyes betrayed his rebellious nature. Formerly a delinquent inner-city youth, he was a fervent anti-establishment adult. Like the dark-eyed lover in rocker Chuck Berry's rowdy song, Dick was my "brown-eyed handsome man."

In *Bluets,* the essayist Maggie Nelson observes: "There are those . . . who like to look. And we have not yet heard enough, if anything, about the female gaze. About the scorch of it." I marked the passage with an asterisk; I recognized that gaze and its heat as my own.

When we first met, when I fell in love, was it the slender build, or the resonant baritone voice, or the rakish goatee—or had he wooed me with those eyes?

≈

One day, the verses were gone. I prompted him with the Thomas: *When I was a windy boy . . . .* He couldn't continue. Instead, he recited a new "ditty," as he called it: *When I was a young lad courting the girls, I looked for my love, and I found her.*

Gradually, he elaborated on the story: *When I was a young man, courting the girls, I saw her. I walked and I walked and I walked and I walked. I caught up to her, put my arms around her, turned her around, and we kissed.* His tale always ended there, with a kiss.

I'd ask, "Who was that woman?"

"You!" he'd declare as he looked at me with delight.

IN THE EVENING, WE'LL DANCE

He told that story quite often for several years. The opening, *When I was a young man,* signaled we'd entered the world of "once upon a time." As he repeated the words *I walked and I walked and I walked and I walked,* his ditty began to resemble a folk tale.

≈

Folk tales help us to shape a narrative self and find our "place in the world," as the scholar Jane Armstrong observes. Was Dick searching for his place in the world as dementia slowly erased his past memories? Perhaps he was shaping a new narrative self to make some sort of meaning out of his changed life.

The protagonist in folk tales leaves home and enters uncharted territory. He or she does this in order to complete a task or, in the folklorist Jack Zipes' words, "fulfill a lack." Dick found much wanting as his memory and cognitive abilities waned; his despair, fury, neediness, and silences told me so.

Casting himself in the role of the seeker, Dick sent himself on his journey to find "her." In his tale, Dick leaves the realm of the known. It's as if he'd embarked on an initiation ritual. The initiate departs, abandoning his past as he begins the task of restructuring his identity. Anthropologists describe this rite of passage as "liminal." *Limen* means *threshold* in Latin. In telling his tale, perhaps Dick intuited that he had stepped over a threshold from a known to an unknown world.

With his slow repetition of *I walked,* I felt his plodding, dogged pace. His was a lonely quest. Dick *walked and walked* in search of *her.* During his journey, the protagonist in folk tales has an encounter with a mysterious being who can be either an enemy or an ally. Dick's tale includes such an encounter: *I caught up to her, put my arms around her, turned her around.*

At this moment, the listener is held in suspense. What would she do? Fortunately, Dick met an ally—me. I would accompany him through adversity. As he wandered in the alien land called dementia, Dick would turn to me again and again, needing assistance and reassurance, seeking the simple gift of love.

The folktale usually ends with the traveler's return home. As the scholar Maria Tatar observes, the most important part of the quest is not attaining power or riches but, having lost one's bearing, finally finding "a way out of the woods back to the safety and security of home." When Dick found me, he'd arrived home.

CHAPTER 3

Wally and Ruth Are in Mexico

In the midst of his dementia, Dick seemed to sense the deep connections that he and I retained for our past loves. "Wally and Ruth are in Mexico," he'd declare. I'd remind him that Ruth, his first wife, had visited Mexico but lived in Minneapolis—and that she was not married to Wally.

Wally, my former lover, resided with his wife in California. Days later, Dick would announce, "Wally and Ruth are in New Mexico." He couldn't seem to pin them down.

≈

The Russian language has a pair of words— *polyubit'* and *razlyubit'*—for falling into and out of love. English doesn't have such a concise way of putting it.

Polyubit': Dick and Ruth met and married in their twenties. They were attractive, bright, and idealistic. They debated politics and Plato, listened to jazz, and danced. They were young. They were ardent. And they were fierce.

Razlyubit': Then, over a span of just four years, Jenny, Anna, and Joe were born. Ruth felt isolated in the suburbs with three small children. They had little money. She recalls, "We both drank and were very negative." Dick was angry. She was depressed. He'd had affairs; she never felt secure in the relationship. In 1973, she left him after fifteen years of marriage.

≈

Polyubit': During college, I'd had a tempestuous affair with Wally. He wooed me with a note he'd placed in my campus mailbox. In his scrawling script, he'd copied down the final lines from Joyce's *Ulysses*: "I put my arms around him yes and drew him down to me so he could feel my breasts all perfume yes and his heart was going like mad and yes I said yes I will Yes." And I said *yes*.

Wally said *yes*, then *no*, then *yes* again. His salutations and closings always were abrupt: Anne (no "Dear") and Wally (no "Love"). "Always know where the door is," he'd tell me. I got the message.

Razlyubit': We broke up during my senior year, in 1971. After I'd graduated, I ran into one of our professors. He said that he'd thought of Wally and me as two tumbleweeds locked together, flung by the winds, rolling across the prairie. We'd pitched headlong into our love affair, entangled in an ambivalent embrace. Windswept, heedless of our destination, we twirled in a mad waltz. We were young, ardent, and fierce.

≈

Polyubit' and *Razlyubit'*: The two terms are emblematic of a love that erupted and sent Wally and me reeling. And so it was with Dick and Ruth. They coupled, then tumbled through fifteen years of marriage.

"Wally and Ruth are in Mexico." Our loves had gone far away. But in Dick's mind, they were still joined to us by memories of the joyous abandon of *polyubit'* and the heartbreak of *razlyubit'*. His. And mine.

CHAPTER 4

Are We Married?

To marry is to walk together on an uncharted road. Neither Dick nor I could have predicted where it would lead us. As Wendell Berry says in a poem addressed to his wife: "You are the known way leading always to the unknown."

I'd discovered Berry's lines from "In the Country of Marriage" while rehearsing them for a concert in 1990. I still hear the poet's words as music: a hammer dulcimer, a hand drum, and the voices of a small ensemble led by the composer, Malcolm Dalglish.

Berry's paean to marriage gave expression to what I felt; the revelation thrilled me. When we arrived at that passage, I'd lean into the lines. Then I'd dance as I sang the lyrics that followed: "How many times have I come to you out of my head / with joy."

The "you" was my husband. He was my known way—and I his. We came to one another out of our heads with joy. And we led one another into the unknown.

≈

Dick and I first met in Minneapolis in 1973. He was mature, self-contained, indifferent to others' opinions of him—a valuable trait in his work as a journalist. Dick lacked pretense; there was nothing studied or affected about him. He was at ease with himself. That attracted me.

Dick was inquisitive; he loved to learn and to patiently share what he'd learned. He'd taught himself how to cross-country ski, develop photos, recite portions of *The Canterbury Tales* in Middle English, speak some rudimentary French, and build a log house. He enjoyed jazz and opera, films and art, playing tennis, camping, and cooking.

I was an idealistic twenty-four-year-old who'd bounced from one job to another: laundry maid, candle factory worker, billing clerk, editorial assistant, teacher's aide, and secretary. Inspired by the diaries of Anaïs Nin, I dashed off journal entries over breakfast, during breaks at work, and in the evenings. I recorded my dreams, my concerns, and my complaints. Some of those entries seem so callow to me now: mewling over my oily skin, my impossible hair, my premenstrual symptoms.

In many ways, I am no longer she, that woman in her mid-twenties. But there, in those journals dated 1973 to 1976, I find careful observations of others and of nature. I find ruminations on courage and time. On those pages, I'd also given voice to my vulnerability as the lover of a much older man. And I declared that I would love him "even though"— even though I had pangs of doubt and feared the unknown.

≈

By 1981, Dick and I were living in northern Minnesota and had been partners for eight years. We'd seldom discussed marriage, since we'd been committed to caring for his three children during that time. Then Joe, the youngest, graduated from high school. With the last of the kids leaving home, we discussed reaffirming our commitment to one another by marrying. Dick said, "Sure. Let's do it. Why not?" I had my doubts, which I disclosed in my journal and to him.

A large sketch diary served as my journal from 1980 until 1984. It's spiral-bound, with thick, cottony paper yellowed along the outer edges. On July 22, 1980, I confessed, "I have a lot to learn about living. And about loving—what it means, does—the action of loving in my life." Later on in the journal, another passage echoes that idea: "It's one thing to espouse an ideal and another to *embody* it." I wanted to embody love and to enact it.

I wrote about my fear of falling out of love. I mentioned the difference in our ages. He was forty-eight; I was thirty-one. I declared, "Dick is not perfect," and wondered, "Can I accept his humanness?" I noted my hesitations about commitment, which I defined as "devoting oneself unreservedly; to pledge; to bind." I considered the seriousness of marriage and the finality of such a commitment: until death. In my dictionary, the word *commitment* is followed by *committal*, a burial.

≈

The rest of the journal contains a miscellanea: my ideas for poems, etymologies of words, observations from our women artists' gatherings, and sketches I'd made of roadside wildflowers (bedstraw, buttercups, sweet rocket, anemone). I mentioned books I'd read (*Akenfield*, *Silences*, *The Snow Leopard*), and a book I resisted reading (*The Denial of Death*). On two pages, I'd stapled the program for a performance of Handel's *Messiah* and a flier for a Seamus Heaney reading I'd attended. Some pages held clippings of amusing newspaper articles. On others, I'd copied out quotations from Katherine Mansfield, Theodore Roethke, Walt Whitman, Sartre—and, near the end of the book, a poem by Seng-ts'an: "One in all / All in one— / If only this is realized / No more worry about your not being perfect."

≈

Then, on a page dated January 8, 1981, two dreams appear, one immediately following the other. The first dream ended with a blunt message, in which a friend told me, "You just want to marry Dick so you can let yourself go to pot. You want him to take care of you. Marriage will ensure that."

After that entry is another, which I call my "marriage dream." The content of the two dreams replicated my wavering. The second dream yielded the answer. I thought it was auspicious. The dream seemed emblematic, a tale from my truest self. Its weightiness overwhelmed the pettiness of the first dream.

My marriage dream is recorded in black ink, in a firm, angular script:

This dream seems to take place in the past. In it, Dick and I walk up a gently sloping mountain. The soft greens of spring unfurl in the trees and shrubs that line the path. We are on our way to get married. We wear red robes trimmed with gold. As we travel up the mountain, we are joined by friends. Colorful ribbons and flowing scarves brighten their plain homespun clothes. They carry flowers and picnic baskets.

We hold the wedding in a small wooden building. The ceremony is brief, solemn, yet joyful. We repeat our vows: "I marry this no-one." Afterwards, we celebrate with singing and dancing.

Over the years, I'd told the story of my marriage dream many times but forgot those enigmatic vows altogether. When I came upon my old journal entry, the vows startled me. How could I have failed to remember them? A better question might be, "Why did I forget them?" Perhaps it's because I didn't understand them at the time.

The meaning of my dream-vows gradually unfolded for me during my husband's decline. I finally fathomed those words, "I marry this no-one." Near the end of his life, at times Dick's ego-self receded and he would become self-less—a "no-one."

≈

We were married in the small log home we'd built by hand. In the wedding photos, we stand in front of a wall of rough pine logs lined with books. We're dressed in long-sleeved, dark-colored clothes, for it was October. A few family members and friends were in attendance. Our dog and cat wandered among the guests. The groomsman had butchered a pig for the wedding feast. It roasted on a spit outside while our friend Larry, a Lutheran minister, conducted the ceremony.

In one picture, the minister's grey-suited back is to the camera. Dick and I face one another. Our bodies frame my grandparents' wedding photograph, placed on a shelf behind us—a wonderful happenstance, a lineage of marriage. My hands wrap around a small bouquet. I'm smiling. Dick stands stiffly erect, his face concentrated and serious.

"What a good thing," I think now, "that he was so serious and present"—because his first marriage had ended in divorce. As we spoke our vows, Dick was resolute; this marriage would not fail.

As his dementia worsened, Dick would ask me, "Are we married?" Sometimes he'd add, "I love you. We should get married."

IN THE EVENING, WE'LL DANCE

≈

Like the rustic site of the ceremony and the plainness of our attire, our vows, too, were simple. A vow is a solemn promise. The origins of the word are in the Latin *votum*, a promise to a god.

Dick and I decided that the traditional marriage vows said what we wanted to say.

In front of witnesses, we affirmed that it was our intention to share our joys, our sorrows, and all that the years would bring. Dick cupped my hands in his, we looked one another in the eyes, and we each pronounced these words: *"I love you and take you to be my husband/my wife. These things I promise you: I will be faithful to you and honest with you; I will respect, trust, and care for you; I will share my life with you, for better or for worse, for richer or for poorer, through sickness and health, till death do us part."*

≈

To love is to "stay with," even if our first and strongest impulse is to run, declares Clarissa Pinkola Estes, a Jungian psychoanalyst. Some stay with. But some must leave because they can no longer endure the drinking, the abuse, the lies, or the loneliness of a union grown empty, drained of love.

I had stayed with Dick for decades before the dementia. Might I have left during his decline had I not been so much younger than Dick? Had I not had such stamina? Would I have stayed with him throughout those seventeen years of dementia if he had not been such a kindhearted husband? I don't know.

I do know that I remained in love with my husband and he with me. I wouldn't run. I chose to "stay with" until death parted us.

≈

Our marriage vows were solemn. We spoke of respect, trust, and health, and of sorrows, sickness, and death on that October afternoon. We faced the unknown knowing that we had devoted ourselves to one another.

In a collection of essays entitled *Standing by Words*, Wendell Berry writes, "The meaning of marriage begins in the giving of words. We cannot join ourselves to one another without giving our word." Dick and I were readers and writers, people of the word. We understood what it meant to stand by words.

We spoke our vows. Then we sealed them with a kiss.

CHAPTER 5

Kiss, Kiss

A wedding gift foretold our lives in ways that Dick and I could not have imagined. Harry, the groomsman, gave us a pine box with dovetailed corners because we'd admired it. He'd carved the story of Rapunzel on its sides and lid, inspired by the writings of Carl Jung and Bruno Bettelheim.

Three decades after our wedding, I read a collection of classic fairy tales. The story that most struck me was "Rapunzel." Over the years, I'd retained only two images from it, both implausible: a doorless tower and Rapunzel's remarkably long hair. Why did that story suddenly resonate with me?

The tale mirrored our marriage. Themes such as song, desire, blindness, and revelation are threaded through that story and ours. The Rapunzel story reassured me that I was not alone and that our journey had meaning.

"Rapunzel" is about much more than a rope of hair, a tower, and a witch. It reminds us that our life stories include trials and transformations. It reminds us that love asks much of us.

≈

Harry had labeled each panel of the box with a Roman numeral to mark the tale's sequence. He chose to depict the Grimm brothers' version. "Rapunzel" has a long history, with many variations from Italy, France, Germany, and England. Some scholars attribute its origins to the legend of Saint Barbara, who was locked in a tower by her father. Folklorists categorize "Rapunzel" as a "Maiden in the Tower" tale.

The most familiar rendition of the story was written by the Grimm brothers. The one I refer to, though, is a much less well-known version found in their 1812 collection of fairytales. It's the first iteration and was written for adults. In it, the prince impregnates Rapunzel during his visits to her tower room. Later, the Grimms revised and edited the story to be suitable for children. That's the variant most people know, often via cartoons and children's storybooks. The adult version is an erotic tale of sexual awakening.

I. Rampion ~ Desire
On one of the end panels, Harry had carved the words "Rampion ~ Desire" above four bell-shaped flowers atop long, slender leaves.

A pregnant woman craves a leafy green called *rampion* (in English) or *rapunzel* (in German). It's a type of bellflower. Both the roots and leaves are edible. Her husband climbs over a high garden wall to steal some for her. He's caught by a crone called Mother Gothel, a German term for a godmother. (In other versions, she's referred to as an ogress, a fairy, a sorceress, or a witch.) It's her garden. The husband explains his pregnant wife's craving and begs the crone's understanding. She spares the man. He can gather the rapunzel—if he promises to give the newborn baby to her.

Desire propels the plot of "Rapunzel": a pregnant woman's desire for the rampion greens, a crone's desire for a child, a prince's desire for Rapunzel, and hers for him. Like a poem, there's a compression in the telling. We learn nothing of the years from the moment Mother Gothel takes the newborn infant until the child reaches the age of twelve, when Mother Gothel imprisons her in the tower. We know that the prince climbs up the rope of her hair, but we don't learn what goes on once he enters her tower room. We can surmise: Rapunzel is a young maiden; suddenly, she's pregnant. And we know this only if we read the version written for adults.

≈

The love between Rapunzel and the prince and between Dick and me began—as most loves do—in sexual yearning. When Dick and I first set eyes on one another, an almost palpable lust thrummed between us.

Although we think of lust solely as sexual desire, originally it referred to any source of pleasure or delight. In that sense, the lust that Dick and I felt for one another endured even as his dementia progressed. We delighted in one another, and we still took pleasure in tender touches and kisses.

"Kiss, kiss," Dick would request, then purse his lips. When words began to elude him, he once said, "A little mouth on my mouth?"

"Do you mean you want a kiss?"

He did.

≈

In 2016, six months after Dick's death, the drummer at a Chicago jazz club caught my eye. I watched him, only him, during the first set. What enthralled me about his drumming was its joyful male energy. It reminded me of my late husband so much that it made my body sing. I retreated to the restroom, where I sat in a cramped stall and wept with yearning and loss.

I mourned the loss of my husband, but I admit that I also craved the carnality, the passions that we'd enjoyed together. I longed for the way he used to lay his eyes, lips, and hands on me.

Rapunzel
The story's title is carved on the back of the box.

Mother Gothel takes the infant from her parents as soon as she is born. She promises to care for her as a mother would. Because the girl's mother had desired the rapunzel greens, Mother Gothel names the child Rapunzel.

I've never had a child, so I've not named one. But if I'd had a girl, I would have named her Anna, after both grandmothers. I'd been christened with a variant of their names, Anne-Marie. Then I met Dick, who had custody of his three children. It delighted me to learn that the younger of the two daughters was named Anna. I got my wish after all.

II. Trumpet Vine ~ Union

On the front panel, three faces emerge from the box's pine wood. In the center is a woman whose hair transmutes into a vine. This is Rapunzel. An old woman looks over her shoulder, open-mouthed, alarmed: the crone. Rapunzel peers down, toward the bottom of the panel, at the face of a man: the prince. His hands are carefully crafted. One clasps a long vine that curves up toward Rapunzel. The other hand reaches out toward a second vine.

When Rapunzel turns twelve, the crone moves her to a tower in the middle of a woods. The tower has neither stairs nor doors, just a solitary window. Rapunzel passes the time by singing to herself. Her songs waft out the tower window and float through the forest. The prince hears her voice as he rides through the woods. He's enchanted. He returns every day, drawn by her song.

He waits. He watches. And then he witnesses the crone calling up to Rapunzel, "Let down your hair." Plaited tresses spill from the window and drape down the tower wall: a rope for the crone. As darkness falls, the prince calls up to Rapunzel. She unwittingly lowers her long locks, assuming it's Mother Gothel waiting in the dark below.

≈

The implausibility of that rope of hair may have prompted Harry to depict a more realistic means of ascent: a trumpet vine. It was an apt choice. The sturdy, woody vine grows rapidly, climbing up to forty feet.

The vine is named for its trumpet-shaped flowers, which symbolize messengers and speech. This, too, is fitting. Rather than sight, it is the sound of songs that draws the prince to Rapunzel. The prince climbs the vine; he wants to see the singer. When he steps through the tower window, Rapunzel is startled. She's never seen a man. He brings her messages of life beyond the tower.

The Grimm brothers' story has the prince wooing her with kindness. He speaks to her of his love. Others say that he seduces her. After all, he is more worldly than she.

In some versions of the tale, the prince offers to marry Rapunzel and she accepts, for her heart is filled with "all the love she could possibly feel for this prince."

≈

I was wooed by Dick's eyes. He stood across the room and turned to greet me. It was love at first sight. The French phrase for this phenomenon is a *coup de foudre*, a lightning strike—an expression that best describes that feeling's force. I knew that I'd met my beloved. It sounds naive, so unlike the jaded, mistrustful woman I actually was. Thus began a union that lasted forty-two years.

III. Hawthorn ~ Despair

This small end panel shows a falling man, hands flung out, eyes closed. Thorn-covered jagged branches—like lightning bolts—surround him.

Night after night, the assignations in the tower continue—until Mother Gothel discovers their secret. The pregnant Rapunzel naively wonders why her clothes have grown so tight. Furious at the betrayal, the crone chops off Rapunzel's hair—a symbolic cutting of the umbilical cord, as one folklorist notes. Then Mother Gothel exiles her. Cast out from the care of the crone, Rapunzel leaves her childhood behind. While in exile, she becomes a mother, bearing twins, a girl and a boy.

The very night of Rapunzel's banishment, the prince calls once again. Mother Gothel lowers the long braid, which she's fastened to a window latch. He climbs up and is shocked to see the crone.

"Rapunzel is lost to you forever," she hisses. In grief and despair, he jumps from the tower, falls into a bramble patch, and is blinded by the thorns.

For years, the blind prince wanders the woods. Lost, he laments the loss of his Rapunzel.

This is the part of the story that first resonated with me. In it, the thorns of tribulation pierce through the gossamer veil of fairytale. This is the part of the story where songs become lamentations, where joys become trials. This is the story of falling—falling from a tower and falling from grace. This is the story of sundered lovers who wander in the world, seeking and suffering.

Like Rapunzel and the prince, Dick and I fell in love. We married. Our love stayed true. Then my husband fell ill, and it felt as if we'd fallen from grace—cast out from our idyll by dementia. Like the blind prince, Dick found himself in a pathless place as dementia shuttered his memories and dimmed his mind.

Dementia resembles a "slow nightfall," words the author Jorge Luis Borges used to describe his failing vision. First, memories blur. Grey shadows crowd the mind. Later, objects grow vague. They're unrecognizable because the names are gone. Night falls.

When I moved my husband to a care facility two years before his death, he was confined, like Rapunzel. The door to the place was locked so the residents couldn't wander away. I'd punch in a code to enter.

Dick would sing to himself to while away the time, as Rapunzel had. One day, an aide saw him sitting alone, singing "You Are My Sunshine." She withdrew to the office and cried.

The image of my husband—forlorn, comforting himself with the song he would often sing to me—harrows me with its loneliness. It grieves me still.

The period of exile is central to the development of both Rapunzel and the prince. Their trials prepare them to move beyond trysts in a tower to a greater maturity.

Rapunzel is banished to a "desert place," a desolate land. It is there that she matures into womanhood. She grows strong as she nurtures her two infants.

While Rapunzel stoically subsists in the wilderness, the blind prince wanders. He lives through a period of aimlessness and emerges as a man, fit to be a husband and father.

Like Rapunzel, I stayed resolute and grew stronger through our trials. Dick remained a loving husband and father, even as he roamed in dementia's wastelands. At times, he would cease his wandering and slip into an inner world. There, he was still and at peace.

IV. Raspberry ~ Revelation

In the center of the lid, two hands reach toward each other, while branches with raspberries, leaves, and flowers twine around them.

The blind prince wanders for a long time, "weeping and wailing" over the loss of his love. Then he hears Rapunzel singing. He follows the sound. It was song that drew them together, and it is song that reunites them.

She gathers him into her arms. In the Grimms' account, the reunion of Rapunzel and the prince is wordless. Instead of speaking, she weeps in compassion, shedding tears onto the prince's eyes. The web of scars dissolves; sight is restored. He opens his eyes and sees his beloved. A revelation.

There's a gap between the two hands that Harry carved into the lid. The gesture reminds me of Michelangelo's "The Creation of Adam." The First Man reclines on the earth. He looks up at the face of God. Their outstretched hands reach toward one another, index fingers almost touching.

In both the painting and the carving, there's a tension in that gap between the hands, like the silence between two musical chords. In that space between, we sense a longing: for the spark of life, for one's love.

But the love I'm thinking about isn't the happily-ever-after kind. It's a love that asks much of us. It's unwavering, compassionate, and strong. It gives us the courage to be led into the unknown, like Rapunzel and the prince were. As Dick and I were.

Hands reach for and find one another. They clasp, united.

≈

Rapunzel and the prince return to his kingdom, where they are greeted with great rejoicing. As is usual in fairy tales, they lived happily ever after.

Three years before his death, Dick announced, "It all comes out well."

"What does?" I asked.

"Our lives."

CHAPTER 6

We Built It

Our lives together mainly took place in "the mulch of the actual," as the critic James Wood puts it. Dick and I were sensible and grounded. Like the leaves we'd heap over perennials in the fall, that "mulch of the actual" enriched us.

Early in our relationship, we'd made choices that prepared us to persevere through the years of dementia. Not that we'd had any foresight. We didn't want to live for a future that might never come to pass. For this reason, we seized the days. Nothing in life is secure, we agreed. If this was true, what was the point of piling up riches? What was the point in deferring our dreams?

So we moved away from the excesses of the city—the traffic, noise, crowds, and consumerism. *"Demasiado,"* we'd say. Too much. We left the Twin Cities in 1978 and migrated to northern Minnesota, settling on twenty acres of lowland.

That was where we chose to be. That was how we chose to be, inspired by Thoreau, Emerson, and friends who had moved back to the land. We wanted to walk as lightly on the earth as we could.

≈

More than forty years ago, we'd paced the outlines of our house in a snow-filled pasture rimmed by woods. Dick's long stride marked out the yards. He counted aloud, and I followed, toe-to-heel, filling in the rectangle. Then we stood off to one side and took in the faint shape, so small in the pasture's sweep and curve. A few fir broke through the grey parallels of aspen. The balsam soughed in the wind, like hooded monks chanting vespers. Low light slipped between leafless trees, casting lavender shadows that draped the snow.

We let the sun guide the design of our house out of respect for the cold, for on the coldest days the sky usually will be clear. We imagined a log cabin with a shed roof, a high south wall of windows capturing the winter sun. We wanted to watch the sun span the sky as it snugged low to the southern horizon in the winter, then swung overhead at summer's height. We wanted to be aware of the world.

We sought a balance of body and mind, working with our hands while living in a home brimming with books. We'd fill milk cans with water from the mudroom pump and haul them inside, aware of the great weight of water, as well as its limpid beauty. In winter, we'd split wood for our cast iron stove. I'd balance a chunk of birch or ash atop a squat stump and make a mental jot on the log's top. The maul fell of its own weight. The jot widened into a crevice and the log cleaved—if my eyes and mind held steady.

≈

We chose to construct a home and a life together. We chose to live simply and attentively, drawing water and chopping wood. Our lives in the cabin's compact quarters were intimate and elemental, the paths to

IN THE EVENING, WE'LL DANCE

the outhouse and woodpile well-worn. We adjusted to the vagaries of weather—winter's profound cold and snowstorms, followed by spring rains and washed-out roads.

We planted a windbreak of balsam and red pine and dug up sod to shape gardens. In the autumn, we harvested wild rice and butchered a pig. We felled trees for firewood in winter's deep snows. In summer, we gardened and picked wild raspberries from the bushes that rimmed our yard. We gathered in small pleasures. We chose to live for today rather than for some imagined future.

≈

One year before his death, Dick asked me, "Is the house holding together?" He was referring to the log cabin. It had been seven years since the need for caregiving aid compelled us to sell the cabin and move into town.

"It is," I assured him.

"Yes," he replied. "We built it."

≈

We shared two main dreams: to build a simple log home and to live abroad for at least a year. In 1988, we left Minnesota to work as English instructors in Madrid, Spain. Surrounded by strangers in a strange place, we felt dislocated and overwhelmed. What seemed like babble swirled around us when we first arrived. We knew some Spanish—but not Castilian Spanish, and not spoken *rápido*.

Our ears, attuned to the hush of our log home, strained to hear one another's voices beneath Madrid's din of traffic noise and alien chatter. Our eyes, accustomed to woodlands and star-strewn night skies, adjusted to a dizzying farrago of city streets and storefront signs: *panadería, joyería, zapatería*. We walked the city for days, orienting ourselves.

≈

During those years we did not envision—could not have envisioned—that we were in training for what was to come. Then the weight of

35

dementia fell. We needed to construct yet another new life. We had to orient ourselves to this alien reality and find ways to apprehend it. We knew how to live with uncertainty. We knew how to live with the raw and the rude, the piss and the shit, as well as the simple and the sublime. We'd seize the days to come as best we could.

Our way of living in the world became our way of living with dementia.

CHAPTER 7

I Still See in the Eyes of My Wife. Beautiful!

Dick's eyes appear intense and watchful in old photographs. I can discern the incisive mind behind them. His eyes also could be amused, skeptical, soulful, or tender. That tenderness is what my Aunt Inez observed years ago at a family dinner. She looked across the table at Dick and exclaimed, "Anne-Marie, I know why you fell in love with Dick! He has the kindest eyes."

References to eyes and sight wend their way throughout these essays. Like a night walker glancing into lit windows and imagining the lives inside, we can glean the inner state of others from their eyes. Recent research confirms that the eyes give us "direct access to another person's inner state," according to Tobias Grossmann, a cognitive scientist. How do they do that? One theory is that genes responsible for the development of the iris also play a role in the frontal lobe, an area of our brains that shapes our personalities.

Both children and adults believe that the self resides in the eyes, not the head, according to a 2012 Yale University study. Even as toddlers we "appear to glean emotional information" from others' eyes. In fact, by the time we're fourteen months old, our "gaze follows eyes almost exclusively," notes Grossmann.

≈

I'd taped a portion of a painting by Georges de la Tour, *The Fortune Teller*, on my office door at the local college where I taught English. It detailed the upper half of a young woman's face, from her brown eyes and fair eyebrows to her high forehead and the white scarf that sheathed her hair. It was cropped that way when I'd found it; that intrigued me.

The young woman peers out of the far corners of her eyes, revealing much of the stark white sclera. Several students told me that it seemed as if her eyes followed them when they walked by my office.

I'd hoped that posting la Tour's young woman on my office door would send a message to my composition students: *Be observant. Keep your eyes open.* It reminded me of the old idiom: "Keep your eyes peeled."

"Keep your eyes peeled, girls," Dad called out to my sister and me as we lolled in the back seat of the Chrysler. We were on the road to the family cottage. Linda and I sat up and peered out the car windows. We vied to be the first to spy Lake Minnewaska's waters beyond the rolling moraines of Glacial Lakes State Park. We'd shout, "I see the lake!" when we glimpsed its silvery shimmer.

On those trips to the lake, Mother would join us in gazing at the countryside. She'd exclaim, "Look!" *Look at the meadowlark. Oh, look! Do you see those dark clouds to the west? Look! A rainbow!* I still carry her counsel with me: Observe the red-winged blackbird, perched on a cattail. See that ravel of clover, aster, and yarrow jostling in the ditch. Look! Keep your eyes wide open.

≈

We now know that our eyes gather in light rays. However, people in ancient Greece held the opposite to be true. They believed that "a visual current was projected outwards from the eye, onto objects," explains the biochemist Rupert Sheldrake. The Greeks thought that eyes possessed great force and were imbued with special powers, such as the malevolent curse of the "evil eye."

The eyes of Lynceus, a mythic Argonaut, had the power to see through skin, as well as walls, trees, and the ground. The eyes of some comic book heroes also have special powers. Superman possesses x-ray vision, depicted either as lightning bolts or as spotlight-shaped cones beaming from his eyes.

Eyes have long been equated with light and the sun, which traditionally are emblematic of intellect, understanding, and spirit. The mythic "all-seeing" giant Argus Panoptes, Hera's faithful watchman, had one-hundred eyes. A multiplicity of eyes is symbolic of vigilance, like the stipple of stars watching over our slumber.

≈

"The mirror is a worthless invention. The only way to truly see yourself is in the reflection of someone else's eyes."
—Voltaire

People turn to mirrors in order to see themselves as others see them, presuming that a mirror reflects a true image of the surface self. They believe that the mirror doesn't deceive. In "Snow White," the vain queen asks her magic mirror, "Who is the fairest of them all?" For years, the mirror replies that it is she. Over those years, Snow White, the queen's stepdaughter, blooms into a beauty. There comes a day when the mirror declares Snow White to be the fairest, much to the aging queen's ire.

We cannot deny the mirror's message. As Sylvia Plath tells us in her poem "Mirror," "I am silver and exact. / I have no preconceptions. . . . / I am not cruel, only truthful."

≈

Persons who have dementia will mirror the emotions of those around them. They'll mimic their gestures and facial expressions. They also catch others' moods. This is referred to as emotional contagion, which "appears heightened in people with Alzheimer's," according to a 2013 study. One of the study's authors, Virginia Sturm, a neuropsychologist, said, "We think some people [with dementia] may have an increased sensitivity to other people's emotions." In an article by the medical journalist Steven Reinberg, Sturm notes that the loss of memory and thinking abilities seems to enhance "other emotional processes." Someone who has dementia may pick up on caregivers' fear, anxiety, or anger—as well as their positive emotions, such as happiness or serenity.

The Flemish novelist Erwin Mortier wrote a memoir about his mother, who had dementia. He states: "She has become a mirror. . . . If the worries and grief are written on our faces, she too is overcome by sadness." He senses that she "scans for all signs of emotion, in my face, in my whole body."

Mortier also observes that if he acted more cheerful than he felt, she'd pick up "the fact that I am behaving differently than my mood dictates." I believe that Dick did this, too. More than once, he'd asserted that I wasn't me: "There are two Annies. You're not the one. You're not Anne-Marie Erickson. Go away!" I suspect that he saw through my guise when I masked my anger or wore a cheery smile even though I felt sad.

Like Plath's mirror, the person with dementia isn't being cruel, only truthful.

≈

During Dick's dementia, my sense of self seemed distorted, like a reflection in a funhouse mirror. I was thrown off-kilter by fear and bewilderment, as if I, too, were trapped in dementia's warped mirror.

Some people with dementia can no longer recognize themselves in mirrors. A friend told me that after her husband developed Alzheimer's, she had to cover the bedroom mirror with a towel. His own reflection frightened him.

Dick had a similar experience. We were in a hotel room in Duluth. Suddenly, I heard a yell from the bathroom. I couldn't catch what Dick had said, so I went to him. He was standing in front of a full-length mirror on the door, glaring at his own reflection. He barked, "Get out of the way" to the stranger in the mirror.

Seeing their likeness can be confusing for persons who have dementia. They may not recognize the reflection as their own and think it's another person, as happened with Dick. Perhaps the unfamiliar hotel room was disorienting, so he and his reflection felt out of place.

Dick never had such a reaction at home. One morning, he called to me: "Annie, come here and see my smile!" I found him standing in front of the bathroom mirror, grinning. My reflection grinned back at him.

IN THE EVENING, WE'LL DANCE

≈

Another's eyes "take us in" and reflect ourselves back to us. The idea of mirroring another harkens to a time before mirrors were invented. Then, "we could not witness ourselves, except with difficulty in pools of water, [and for this reason] we needed others to see us, to make us visible," explains essayist Alexandra Kleeman.

To mirror another is to faithfully reflect him or her. Thus, the person mirrored perceives an echo of his or her self, like sound waves rebounding off walls and reverberating back to a listener.

Some people lack a clear sense of self, so psychotherapists may use mirroring to reflect and affirm them. Mirroring can help persons with dementia preserve a sense of self, even though they've lost their memories and social identities. They need others to see them, to reflect them, to make them visible to themselves. I made a practice of reminding Dick of who he was by mirroring him.

"There are two ways of spreading light: To be the candle or the mirror that reflects it," notes the novelist Edith Wharton. I became the mirror reflecting Dick's inner light. Near the end of his life, he said, "I still see in the eyes of my wife. Beautiful!"

≈

Idioms about eyes and sight abound, indicative of the powers we attribute to them. When we're in agreement with someone, we "see eye-to-eye." When we're empathetic, we "see through the eyes" of another. And when we say, "I see," we mean, "I understand."

There are at least fifty synonyms for *to see*, including *gaze*. The long, intent look of a gaze is a form of communion between the viewer and the viewed, the act of seeing and being seen. As Karl Ove Knausgaard observes in an essay, "In the gaze of the other, we become, and in our own gaze others become."

The word *behold* resembles the communion implicit in a gaze. Richard Rohr, a theologian, observes that *to behold* is to be "present to what is . . . completely enchanted by something outside and beyond yourself."

When we behold, we allow someone or something "to reveal its inherent dignity, as it is," says Rohr. We watch over and cherish that person or thing. Thus, I beheld my husband. And he beheld me.

≈

My cousin Patricia commented on a photo of Dick and me: "What I see in that wonderful picture is a reflection of your gentle spirit on his face." But the mirroring was not one-way. His spirit was reflected on my face, as well.

I looked him in the eyes and told him that he was my brown-eyed handsome husband.	*He looked me in the eyes and told me that I was his blue-eyed beautiful wife.*
I looked him in the eyes and told him, "You are a kind and gentle man."	*He looked me in the eyes and told me, "You are so kind and so fond."*
When his eyes met mine, I'd tell him, "You're my love, my one true love."	*When my eyes met his, he'd tell me, "I love you more than words can say."*

≈

The philosopher Martin Buber's *I-Thou* is a "turning toward," an affirmation of the other as he or she is. In that sense, it resembles mirroring. In the *I-Thou* duality, each is being present to the other's unique, whole being. It isn't mystical, but it requires a reverence toward the other. It's a form of grace.

I'd eagerly studied Buber's writings in college and revisited them recently. A phrase of his that I'd never read before struck me. Buber declares that *I-Thou* is "familiar to anyone with a candid heart and courage to stake it."

A "candid heart and courage to stake it": what a remarkable and apt pairing of words.

I-Thou requires a heart that's candid—honest, sincere, and open to the vulnerabilities of love and loss. *I-Thou* means committing one's heart to another person. That's where the courage comes in.

≈

Some family members may have the heart but lack the courage. They might feel that the person with dementia has become a stranger, completely sundered from the person he or she was in the past. They might feel the need to turn away from their loved one, for it seems as if she or he is already "gone."

At times Dick was seemingly gone; often, he was present. Even as he became more *not himself* in some respects—with the loss of memory and abilities—his indwelling being endured. I sought out what remained. And I was surprised by what was gained in the wake of loss. Sometimes, like a guttering flame, an unselfed being would shine out, transcending his ego-self. He was both present and absent, here and gone.

In the first years of Dick's forgetfulness, I saw things dimly. Gradually, living with dementia burned away all my illusions. As the art critic Peter Schjeldahl avers, "Hard light is wanted in a crisis; away with moonbeams." In that hard light I saw things as they really were. And I pledged to bear witness.

≈

After my husband's passing, I searched for images of death to understand how others have envisaged it. I found etchings and paintings of skeletons, skulls, and hooded figures. I found *Death and the Woodcutter*, a powerful depiction by Jean-François Millet, who is best known for his paintings of peasant life. I also discovered Millet's oil painting *Bird's-Nesters*. It was his final work—a "last testament"—painted shortly before his death in 1875. It's a lesson in the seeing of things.

At first glance, *Bird's-Nesters* is difficult to make out, its murky greens and browns limned by a soft gold. A brilliant flash of light, like

Jean-François Millet. *Bird's-Nesters,* 1874.
The William L. Elkins Collection. Philadelphia Museum of Art, 1924

a bolt of lightning, explodes near the center of the canvas. It's a fiery torch, extended toward the sky, held up by a man who's leaping forward, his back toward the viewer. He's holding a club in his right hand, ready to strike. Another man stands next to him. He faces the viewer but looks skyward, mouth agape. One hand clutches a club; the other is raised, palm up. It's as if he's pleading with an apparition. Vague dark figures swarm around the two hunters, like waves in a seething deep-green sea. I looked more closely: the dark shapes are birds, frantically winging above and around the hunters. The canvas itself seems shattered by the ghostly birds, like paint flaking from the cloth.

A dab of red draws the viewer's eyes toward the ground. A woman in a red headscarf crawls on her knees, next to a man. Small black mounds lie scattered on the autumnal stubble: the bodies of birds. The man clutches a bird, its wings raised, beak open in a silent cry.

Millet based this painting on his memories of bird hunts. In Gruchy, the village of his childhood, the peasants hunted pigeons, or doves;

the names of the birds in the family Columbidae often are used interchangeably. Large flocks of pigeons would roost in the trees at night. The peasants startled them awake, blinding them with the sudden, bright torchlight. Then they clubbed the birds to death, slaughtering them for food.

Millet declared that he wanted to disturb the privileged Parisian gallery-goers "in their contentment and leisure." He did. They were shocked by his depictions of the harsh life in rural France. The peasants in Millet's portraits looked to them like "beasts." The public did not want to see them.

≈

In my enthusiasm, I showed a reproduction of the painting to several friends and explained what it depicts. Some would look away. They could see no beauty in it. I thought it was stunning: the dark and the light, the humble and the luminous, the barbarous and the beautiful, all captured in one canvas. As the English artist David Brett observes of *Bird's-Nesters,* "Despite this grisly subject matter, the painting has an ecstatic quality." It enthralled me.

Perhaps the grisliness didn't disturb me because I was used to the sight of dead animals. My father was a butcher; he owned a meat market with my grandfather. They slaughtered cattle at nearby farms. When I was a child, Dad would let me walk into the cold, clean locker to see the large quarters of beef hanging from hooks, their deep-red muscle and ivory fat, their foreshanks dangling downward in a stiff arabesque. I inhaled the sharp smell of chilled beef and blood. I was fascinated.

The American poet Ellen Bass reveals a similar fascination when she hymns the act of butchering chickens in precise, visceral language. She concludes: "I loved the truth. Even in just this one thing: / looking straight at the terrible, / one-sided accord we make with the living of this world."

Both Bass and Millet "look straight" at terrible truths. That was how I eventually chose to live with Dick's dementia. However, some people would avert their eyes when my husband entered a room, the dementia manifest in his slow shuffle and stooped frame. Perhaps they feared dementia or merely felt uncomfortable. Perhaps seeing my husband brought up painful memories of a loved one who had the disorder.

I felt obliged to look straight at the brutal disease that ravaged him because I love the truth, as did Dick.

PART 2

Losing,
Re-Collecting

CHAPTER 8

I'm Making More Mistakes

He was sixty-six and often seemed lost in thought. He'd run his long fingers over the spines of books that lined one wall of our home. He'd caress the rough, stiff fabric of hardcovers, the smooth spines of paperbacks, pausing when he reached a line of Orwellia—the novels, a thick collection of essays, several biographies. Then on to the volumes of political philosophy he had studied in graduate school, bindings and pages brittle with age.

He noted in his agenda book for that year, 1998, that he'd rummaged through some old photos and was "thinking of memoir writing." Did he intuit the need to capture his memories before they began to elude him? A few months later he told me, "I'm making more mistakes. You point them out to me. I'm not objecting to the fact that you do that, but it depresses me. As I get older, I'll be making more mistakes."

≈

Some creatures—such as box turtles, black quahog clams, and red sea urchins—live one-hundred or more years and show few signs of senescence, the usual age-related decline. Spiny sea urchins survive up to a century or two because their telomeres don't shorten as they age, unlike those of humans. Telomeres are the "aging clocks" in our cells. The shorter one's telomeres, the faster one ages biologically. They've been compared to the fuse of a bomb.

We number our years chronologically, one birthday to the next. But those calendar years might not correspond with our biological age, which can be measured by the length of our telomeres. Like the plastic aglets that tip a drawstring to prevent unraveling, telomeres sheathe each end of our chromosomes. They buffer them so they don't fray or fuse with one another. Each time a cell divides, the telomeres grow shorter. Gradually, our cells can no longer divide, and they become inactive, which leads to age-related diseases and, eventually, death.

When I first read about telomeres I was struck by their resemblance to the Fates, mythical goddesses who dictated the length of a life. The Norse called them Norns; in Roman mythology, they're the Parcae, the three goddesses of fate. They control the thread of life, from birth to death. Nona spins the thread; Decima uses a measuring rod to allot the fiber's length. When a mortal's time has come, Morta cuts the life-thread with her shears. The name Morta means "Dead One."

Telomeres are the Decimas of the cellular world. Was the measure of Dick's days dwindling as his telomeres frayed and failed? Did Morta stand ready with her sharp shears?

≈

During his sixty-sixth year and for the previous twenty-five years I'd known him, Dick was inquisitive, engaged, and capable. He still worked as a freelance writer and photographer. He was athletic; he played tennis, biked, jogged, and skied cross-country. Dick moved with vigor as he strode across the yard, tending to the lawn, gardens, bird feeders, and firewood.

But when he was tired, I'd notice the darkness beneath his eyes, the creases at their corners and across his brow. Age shaded his temples. What I could not see were the microscopic lesions caused by abnormal proteins or small strokes—either of which could have been silently compromising his brain.

What created those lesions? How could I know? I couldn't see or hear or touch those silent shape-shifters hidden beneath the bony shield of his cranium.

≈

For the seeker, a key represents possibility: the possibility of finding a treasure or unlocking a mystery. Of course, first the key must be found, as must the door or chest or box to which it fits. The key slips into the lock, it turns—and then—what is found? A treasure? Maybe, if it's a pirate tale. The bodies of murdered wives? That's what Bluebeard's young bride discovers locked in a closet. Or perhaps the room or chest is empty; the hero finds nothing.

Sometimes the key is a word or a phrase. "Open Sesame" is such a phrase, referred to as a "mountain opens to magic" formula by folklorists. It's the expression Ali Baba overhears. He tries it out, commanding "Open Sesame" at the sealed mouth of a cave. It opens; inside lies a treasure stowed away by thieves.

A word uttered to unlock magic, ABRACADABRA, is shouted by the stage magician before he pulls a silk scarf or rabbit from his black top hat. That ancient formula also acted as an incantation to protect against misfortune or disease. Some people wore the letters as an amulet, inscribed in a triangular shape, like a top:

A - B - R - A - C - A - D - A - B - R - A
A - B - R - A - C - A - D - A - B - R
A - B - R - A - C - A - D - A - B
A - B - R - A - C - A - D - A
A - B - R - A - C - A - D
A - B - R - A - C - A
A - B - R - A - C
A - B - R - A
A - B - R
A - B
A

≈

ABRACADABRA! Dick and I loved to spin words around, volley them back and forth, play with them, pun with them. Our own words spilled onto the pages of notebooks and sheaves of paper bearing our articles, reports, editorials, essays, letters. Words—in rows of books and piles of magazines—also served us as keys to knowledge.

I searched for scientific words in medical reports that might unlock the mystery wending its way through my husband's brain. However, the text that seemed most suited to our story was an old folktale. The tale features a key made of gold, a precious metal that symbolizes spiritual powers. It's the final story in the Grimm brothers' 1815 collection.

"The Golden Key" is one paragraph long. In it, a poor boy fetching firewood on a winter's day finds a tiny golden key beneath the snow. He searches further and digs up an iron chest. The key fits the keyhole. He turns the key, unlocks the chest, lifts the lid, "and then we shall learn what kind of wonderful things there were in the little chest. *The End*." Perhaps that's the spiritual power the golden key imparts: the awareness that we cannot know.

When I first read that enigmatic ending, mouth agape with an unspoken *And?*, silence answered me. The key to the mystery of my husband's disease also opened to silence, a silence left in the wake of scientific words tumbling over one another, so many words spilling so swiftly. This week's headlines about the latest research rushed past me, merging with a flood of findings from last month, last year. Still, I discovered no answer. I read. I waited. And? An uneasy silence. Perhaps I could not know.

≈

Nothing in the universe except the universe itself is more complex than the human brain, according to scientists. When it comes to understanding the causes of brain degeneration, we face a conundrum—the box for which we have yet to find a key. In some ways, the workings of the brain remain opaque, despite the MRI images of its interconnected neural tracts, ablaze with color and alive with energy.

Researchers have been seeking a single, simple answer, but there probably isn't just one. And it isn't simple, as much as doctors, caregivers, and the public might wish it were. "No one expects the brain to yield its secrets quickly or easily," observes James Gorman, a science reporter.

Often, I was confronted with the blunt question, "Does Dick have Alzheimer's?"

"Maybe," I'd reply, as anger and sadness churned inside my chest. "Maybe. Who knows?"

That's why I decided to call Dick's disorder "dementia," an umbrella term that describes symptoms, including impaired thinking and memory, but doesn't identify a cause. Because Alzheimer's is the most prevalent form of dementia and the focus of many research studies, it's the label that first comes to mind. The label commonly used until the 1970s was *senile dementia.* Peter Whitehouse, a geriatric neurologist, simply refers to the "aging brain," since we all will lose some cognitive abilities as we age.

I would have considered my husband's memory problems to be normal had he been in his nineties—the age of my grandfather when the family noticed signs of senility. *Senile,* from the Latin *senex,* simply means "old man." Yet Dick was not an old man when he first mentioned his lapses. He was in his sixties.

What I noticed were his checkbook errors. He began to make mistakes in basic math—a man who had been competent at statistical analysis and calculations. While we lived in Madrid, he recorded our expenditures in his 1988 planner. Every day, he'd entered columns of items—a newspaper, a subway ticket, postage stamps—and their cost. Then he tallied them. He also noted our daily activities in a tidy cursive that marched in orderly lines across the pages.

A decade later, in 1998, his planner pages grew haphazard. Instead of neat lines of script, helter-skelter entries began appearing. Some entries were crossed out; they'd been made in error. On December 28 he wrote a note to himself to shoot a photo: "County Board Safety Award pix, 3:05 p.m." Then, "No go / have one." He'd forgotten that he'd already taken it.

A few months later, I scribbled this note into my engagement calendar: "I'm feeling depressed about Dick's lack of energy, aches, forgetfulness—with *no answers* as to why."

≈

The lack of answers didn't stop me from searching for explanations. I wanted at least an illusion of control over my husband's disease. My search resembled Dick's own frustrated groping for words. He'd glance at his wristwatch, but the word *watch* would transform into *mirror*. His knuckles became *nimnits*. "I don't know how to say this exactly, but . . ." he'd begin, then trail off, at a loss for words.

I don't know how to say it, either—to sort through the words that might explain what happened to my husband's brain. I find myself lost in a thicket of theories, hypotheses, and studies.

I read that a diseased brain is often characterized by abnormal protein fragments— neurofibrillary tangles of tau protein inside nerve cells and beta-amyloid protein clumps (also called amyloid-beta or A-beta) outside the cells. But then I learned about the Nun Study and the 90+ Study. Both revealed that an appreciable percentage of people with obvious dementia do not have either the plaques or the tau tangles. And there are people whose memories and cognition remain fully intact, but whose brains are riddled with tangles and plaques. How can that be, if they are the distinguishing feature of dementias? No one knows for sure.

Some researchers theorize that tau malfunction produces the plaques. Others are of the opposite opinion. Do the tangles cause the plaques or do plaques cause tangles? Or perhaps something else is killing nerve cells, and the plaques actually are trying to repair the damage. Perhaps amyloid is "the smoke, not the fire," speculates Scott Small, director of Columbia University's Alzheimer's Disease Research Center.

In 2016, researchers proposed that amyloid might actually be working to protect the brain, creating a "cage" that traps bacteria. Are the tangles and plaques the cause—or are they an effect? I could speculate as to the cause of my husband's dementia, but what can I say today that will not be outdated within a year—or less?

≈

After more than two decades of medical research focused largely on amyloid, some scientists have declared that tau drives the cognitive dysfunction in Alzheimer's. The neurologist Sarah DeVos argues that tau may pose a greater threat than amyloid. In a 2023 overview of Alzheimer's research in *Nature Reviews Neurology*, the authors point out that many of the early attempts to develop treatments for the disease focused on amyloid, "but a lack of efficacy of these treatments in terms of slowing disease progression led to a change of strategy towards targeting of tau pathology."

In an online video about Alzheimer's, illustrations of the tau protein inside the brain's neuron cells are bathed in pleasant pinks and mauves. The interior of the neuron seems a busy place, as tau works to stabilize the tubular structures, called microtubules, that transport nourishment and messages within the cell. Changes in the protein cause threads of tau to disengage from the microtubules; in the animation, it looks like an unzipping. The tau threads fly off and twist together with other threads to form tangles. The tubular structures collapse, causing the neuron to die. It's thought that as the tau tangles accumulate more brain cells are killed, which gradually causes memory failure.

Whether the main culprit is tau or amyloid, most researchers believe that both tau tangles and amyloid plaques contribute to the degradation of nerve cells in the brain. However, the relationship between the two is little understood.

≈

I'd known nothing about either tau or amyloid until I came upon an issue of *Discover* magazine in 2008. I paged through it while waiting at the clinic with Dick. A large, three-D image of an amyloid-beta (A-beta) peptide fibril—the type of protein fragment that accumulates in the brain as plaques—caught my eye. It had been produced by a transmission electron microscope. Shaped like a shuttlecock, black, with a red and yellow flare at one end, it propelled itself across the page. At first glance, it reminded me of an exotic tulip, laid on its side. I tore the page out and tucked it into my purse.

When I looked at it later, I was dumbstruck. What initially appeared benign now seemed sinister. Leech-black, the slimy shape narrows, twists, and then splits, like a cobra's tongue. The fibril seems to fly, sans wings, sans feathers. The idea of a bat flitted into my mind, although the fibril isn't shaped like one. Something about the fibril's blackness, its silent flight, reminded me of being stirred from sleep by the rustling of a bat as it hurtled through our log home. The double-natured bat—part bird, part rat—evoked fear in me. Did fears wing their way through Dick's mind, too, as unease about his mistakes mounted?

Due to its nocturnal habits, many mythologies associate the bat with darkness and mystery. In Buddhism, bats represent darkened understanding, which is an apt description of dementia. In Mayan mythology, a bat-demon, Zotz, swallows the light. The bat-black fibril pictured in that magazine could have been Zotz's misshapen offspring.

The A-beta peptide fibrils actually are misshapen. It's that abnormality that may give birth to Alzheimer's, which has been described as a proteopathic disease. Proteopathy—*proteo* (protein) *pathy* (disease)—refers to diseases in which certain proteins fail to fold into their normal configuration; they are "misfolded." Many neurodegenerative diseases, such as Parkinson's and Huntington's, are caused by wrongly-folded proteins. Advancing age also is a risk factor for increased protein misfolding.

Protein chains form into either the spiral shape of a helix or something called a "beta pleated sheet." The beta protein sheet is puckered; hence, "pleated." Both types of protein then fold to form a 3-D shape in order to function properly. However, if proteins misfold, they lose their normal function. Referred to as "rogue" molecules, they can convert normal molecules into the misfolded form, causing a cascade of transformations.

Misfolded A-beta peptide fibrils clump together to form plaques, which resemble liver spots or melanomas in microphotographs of brain tissue. The sticky plaques can't be cleared by the body. And they are thought to be toxic to nerve cells.

IN THE EVENING, WE'LL DANCE

≈

The word *misfold* does not appear in my dictionary. Immediately before the place where *misfold* would appear I find the word *misfit*, something which is the wrong shape—as is a misfolded protein. The next entry in the sequence is *misfortune.*

Even though the word isn't in my dictionary, I know about *misfolding*. It reminds me of my mishaps as a laundry maid. Before I met Dick, I worked in the laundry at St. Mary's Hospital in Minneapolis while attending college. My job was to fold things: towels, sheets, blankets, pillowslips, and patient gowns. Sometimes the gowns would be fed into a mangle, a machine with heated rollers that presses fabrics. The mangle at St. Mary's was monstrous. It filled a large room, gave off waves of heat, and roared. It was turned off at the end of the day shift; fortunately, except for a regular Saturday stint, I worked nights.

On Saturday mornings when I punched my timecard, I could hear the thing running. I dreaded that mangle, but occasionally the boss would order me to join the line of workers stationed behind the machine. Grey carts piled with damp patient gowns were rolled in next to us. We'd grab a gown, then lay it on the lip of the mangle, quickly flattening the fabric and folding in the sleeves before the gown was grabbed up by the rollers. If my hands weren't adept, the gown would come out the other end misfolded.

≈

Some scientists use the labels "BAPtists" to describe supporters of the beta-amyloid peptide (BAP) theory and "TAUists" when referring to the tau tangle adherents, according to the biochemist Peter Davies. It's as if they were religious sects. Rather than focusing on the plaques or tangles, the neurologist Frank Longo says, "We're agnostic about what is actually causing Alzheimer's." His team is looking at ways to keep brain cells strong.

One tenet that medical researchers can agree on is the impact vascular damage has on the brain. In fact, prior to the focus on tangles and plaques, strokes were considered to be the most common cause of dementia. Dick's initial diagnosis, in 2001, was that small strokes revealed by an MRI probably had caused his short-term memory loss.

The word *ischemia* refers to inadequate blood supply to an organ due to a blood clot. An ischemic stroke occurs when there isn't enough blood flow to an area of the brain. Those cells can't get oxygen. They die. The areas of dead tissue are called cerebral infarcts.

Unlike the scars that form over an injury to our skin, cerebral infarcts—the spaces where tissue is lost—don't fill back in. When brain tissue is examined under a microscope, the infarcts resemble aerial photographs of craters. Infarcts are described as "cavitations," from the Latin *cavus*, meaning a void, a hollow, or a hole.

≈

Both *hole* and *hell* derive from *kel*, an Old English word related to the underworld. The two words are combined in *hellhole*, which is a miserable, wretched place. My grandmother taught me that word. She lived in an old brick tenement in my hometown. Her apartment door faced a side street; the back door of a bar opened onto it. Late at night, she'd be startled awake by drunken yells and brawls. She referred to the bar as "that hellhole." I don't recall its real name; maybe I never knew it. I'd picture men in a dark, smoke-filled room, their brains shriveling with every shot they downed.

Although he probably hadn't spent time in many hellholes, Dick had been a drinker before I met him. Mainly scotch; gin on hot summer days. When he was in his thirties, he noticed a decline in the excellent memory he'd had as a young man. He attributed it to his "drinking days." Although he'd quit drinking when he was forty-one, I wondered if the alcohol already had irreparably damaged his memory.

He told me that several times he'd experienced memory blackouts. He had no recollection of how he'd managed to drive home from a bar. In effect, blackouts caused by intoxication gradually snuff out the lights in a drinker's brain as they disrupt activity in the hippocampus, the brain's memory center. The person's ability to form new memories is impaired; this is called anterograde amnesia. The more alcohol, the greater the memory impairment. Sometimes Dick was so intoxicated, the blackout so complete, that a memory probably didn't form.

Alcohol abuse also can aggravate the natural age-related shrinkage of the frontal lobe, which integrates memories and is involved in problem solving, language, judgment, and other functions. Although some nerve cell loss may be permanent, much of the damage can be reversed with abstinence, thanks to the growth of new neurons (neurogenesis) in areas of the brain, including the hippocampus.

Dick drank alcohol for many years; then he was sober for decades more. What conclusions can I draw? I do know that eventually he was unable to form new memories or recall old ones. His brain may have been damaged by alcohol, riddled with plaques and tangles—or pocked with voids caused by infarcts. Where memories once existed, there was a void.

≈

Infarcts, tau tangles, and plaques are often described as "telltale signs" of various forms of dementia. Something that reveals information is "telltale," which is how the word is used in this case. But the first meaning of *telltale* is "one who informs on another, a talebearer."

Many scientists believe that the damaged plaques and tangles trigger a chain of events that spreads like a rancorous rumor—gradually causing great harm throughout the brain. In that sense, those abnormal proteins resemble a talebearer.

I, too, am a bearer of tales—but with benign intent. For you, the reader, I'm fashioning a narrative of events in the lives of my husband and me. The narrative is as true as I can make it, but when I confront unknowns I resort to conjecture: What might my husband have been thinking? What was happening to his brain?

≈

The essayist Maria Popova discusses ideas presented in *Actual Minds, Possible Worlds* by Jerome Bruner, a psychologist. She concludes that scientific pursuit is concerned with how to know truth, while the storyteller is concerned with the question of how to endow experience with meaning. Bruner explains that both are "ways of knowing." Scientific analysis results in information, whereas stories produce meaning.

I needed both ways of knowing. I turned to science for information, hoping it would reveal truths about the cause of Dick's dementia. And I turned to stories as a way of endowing our experience with meaning.

≈

As the reports on tau and amyloid demonstrate, medical science has produced conflicting evidence and uncertainty. In an intriguing locution, one writer states that there are problems with viewing Alzheimer's as a "stable, locatable 'disease object.'" Its biology, causes, and risk factors still aren't fully understood.

In fact, Paul Rosenberg, a geriatric psychiatrist at Johns Hopkins, argues, "It's probably not one kind of Alzheimer's disease, it's probably many. What we want to do is find the subtypes so we can find better treatments."

Rather than a "one-size-fits-all" strategy, the neurologist Tara Tracy thinks that eventually treatment plans might be created to target tau, beta-amyloid, and other causes. She compares the future of treating neurodegenerative diseases to cancer treatments that can be tailored to each patient's needs. "We need a variety of approaches," she says. "I don't think that there's going to be one thing that cures Alzheimer's."

Donald Weaver, co-director of the Krembil Brain Institute, recently declared, "We need new ways of thinking about this disease." Weaver explained that researchers at the Institute "don't think of Alzheimer's as fundamentally a disease of the brain. We think of it as a disease of the immune system *within* the brain."

Following a comprehensive survey of Alzheimer's history, literature, and research, the medical anthropologist Margaret Lock concluded that "the Alzheimer's phenomenon . . . is a moving target, and so far it has been doggedly resistant to all efforts to neatly define and treat it." For years, I'd suspected as much.

IN THE EVENING, WE'LL DANCE

≈

Despite the many scientific clues, the mystery remains, waiting to be solved. Mysteries, rather, since dementia can take various forms. The medical researcher Jerome Groopman reminds us that "science operates around a core of uncertainty, within which lie setbacks." But, he adds, "also hope."

I struggled to understand this mystery, to make meaning out of the disease that ravaged much of my husband's brain. While he lived, I'd read news reports about research findings, seeking a measure of hope. Then I'd remind myself that Dick was in the last stages of dementia. Any potential cure would be too late for him.

Emily Dickinson tells us that "hope is the thing with feathers." My heart held scant perches for hope. I hoped my husband would continue to recognize me. I hoped that he would remain comfortable and content. I hoped that he would die before he reached a vegetative state. And I summoned up hope that someday soon a cure would be found for those in the earliest stages of dementia.

Unlike the poet's bright-feathered birds, my hopes seemed small, like dun-colored sparrows sheltering in a shrub. For Dick, the trees were barren of birds. They'd flown away. As his sense of past and future vanished, so, too, did his capacity for hope—since hope hovers ahead of us, in the future.

Hope can sustain patients and their families through a disease. With hope, we can, as Groopman suggests, "see—in the mind's eye—a path to a better future." But he cautions that hope needs to be "rooted in unalloyed reality." It can't be a thing in flight. It must be anchored, its toes wrapped firmly around a sturdy branch as it bobs about in ill winds.

Dementia is a terminal disease. There would be no remission, no cure, no better future for my husband. That was the unalloyed reality.

≈

In 1998—the year when he'd first intuited that something was amiss—Dick played on the floor with Gracie, his three-year-old granddaughter.

They played at being rabbits and piggies. They sang "Ring Around the Rosie."

She chanted: "Ashes, ashes, we all fall down" and collapsed dramatically to the floor. Then she'd giggle, breaking the spell. After a few repetitions of the rhyme, she changed her chant: "We all fall *up*!" She flung her arms upward as she jumped in the air.

Little Gracie would fall up for many more years, while her grandfather—ashes to ashes—slowly fell down.

CHAPTER 9

I'm My Own Person

All I had were my observations over the years of our lived experience. I wanted schema from which I could hang those experiences, like a heap of clothes sorted out and neatly pinned to a clothesline. I read to explore and comprehend our experience. I read articles by ethicists, neuroscientists, medical anthropologists, medical historians, and philosophers.

While I read, I jotted down the definitions of *human, person, identity, self.* I read that "there's no widespread agreement on what a 'self' is," according to philosopher Stephen Millet. I read "Disremembered," an essay by Charles Leadbeater, who posits that people who have a loved one with dementia undergo "a crash-course in the philosophy of mind." That's because philosophy offers insights about selfhood. Those insights can "help us make sense of the condition and our own reactions to it," proposes Leadbeater.

No wonder my reading was so eclectic. I wanted to make sense not only of Dick's condition, but also of his retention of self.

≈

As his disease progressed, I studied Dick's face, trying to read the mutable moods and mysteries of his dementia when language would fail him. I'd translate gestures and scraps of sentences, the look in his eyes, his quietude.

I wanted to validate what I'd observed in my husband: how elements of his self were both retained and transcended through the last years of his life. I'd witnessed the self that remained despite his losses, as well as an unselfing. Our friends saw it, too.

The evidence was there, in my memories, in my many notes, in photographs, and in several videos. In a 2012 video, shot fourteen years into the dementia, he faces me, looks into my eyes, and sings "You Are My Sunshine." His voice is resonant, the pacing brisk. He begins that same song in the winter of 2015—voice clear, eyes downcast—forgets the lyrics after the initial line, pauses, sings "You—," pauses, "remember me."

That July he sings a song he'd invented: "In the end of the day," he falters, then sings in a faint voice, "You are the one, you are the wonder." The skin on his hands is a pale tissue veined in blue. He toys with an invisible thread between his hands.

In the last video, he's seated in his wheelchair, intently scuffling along in his blue-slippered feet, his former stride now reduced to wee steps. His head seems unnaturally large atop his gaunt body, like a child's stick figure. He stops. Coughs. The video is dated October 23, 2015. A week later, he was dead.

≈

I needed to interrogate the *himself/not himself,* the *present/absent,* the concomitant *to be* and *not to be,* of my husband's decline. I was bewildered as to how to proceed, how to find the words to tell you about this paradox. I wanted to relate what I knew, as well as the unknowable. "Language, as we have it, fails to deal with confusion," observes Fanny Howe, a poet and essayist. To be utterly confused is to be bewildered: *be* (thoroughly) -*wilder* (led astray, lost). When we've lost our bearings, our world turns topsy-turvy and orderly boundaries crumble. That's when we might break open "the lock of dualism (*it's this or that*)," says Howe.

So here I am, perched unsteadily on the seesaw's fulcrum. It's not *this*. It's not *that*. It's both this *and* that.

≈

Two photos: One, a studio portrait, was shot when Dick was in his thirties. I took the other when he was eighty-one and in the final stages of dementia. As he aged, his face lost its leanness and softened. But an

air of curiosity, kindness, and amusement remained—along with something new. He glowed.

The poet Anne Carson describes looking at her father, who had dementia. It was like seeing "a well-known face, whose appearance is exactly as it should be in every feature and detail, except that it is also, somehow, deeply and glowingly, strange."

There's clearly some congruence between the two photographs of my husband—just as many aspects of the man who had dementia accorded with the man he'd always been. At least, I believed that was true. I wanted to confirm my perceptions, so I asked people who had known him.

For his memorial service, I'd invited old friends to share memories of Dick prior to his dementia. Notes and cards from others enlarged upon that portrait. I also asked the staff at Oak Hill how they would describe him. When he lived in that facility, from 2013 until his death in 2015, he was in the last stages of the disease, unable to dress or bathe himself, eventually unable to walk or to feed himself.

Sans dementia	**With dementia**
Old friends said he was a good, wonderful, beautiful man, who was gentle, kind, and loyal. They commented on his abiding love for his family and me. Old friends wrote about his humor, irreverence, and quick wit.	*The Oak Hill staff described Dick as thoughtful and loving and mentioned his kind, gentle ways. It was amazing, they said, to witness his unconditional love for me. The Oak Hill staff said that he was humorous.*
Friends said he was an intelligent man capable of incisive analysis and intense, thought-provoking discussions.	*Despite the late stage of his dementia, the staff noted that Dick was "very smart."*
Michael, who had known Dick for many years, described him as "vivid." *Vivid*: vigorous, vital, bright, distinct.	*"Vibrant" was the adjective an Oak Hill aide used—a word that suggests spiritedness and vividness.*
They said he was unique.	*He was eccentric, unconventional.*
One friend declared that "Dick Cain was a powerhouse."	*The staff observed that Dick was determined, obstinate, and strong.*

These consistencies across time were due to considerate caregivers, my steadfast love, and his strong will. Studies have shown that people will strive to retain a sense of self in the face of dementia. It's not uncommon. And Dick always had been resolute. If he was determined to do a thing, he'd usually achieve it. With sheer tenacity, he'd quit smoking and drinking—on his own.

Dick also was, as our friend Michael observed, "fully present." Recently, I came upon an entry in a journal from 1978. I'd described Dick this way: "He is so *there*: so solid, so true, so much himself, in such an exciting, curious, joyful way."

To the end, Dick Cain remained resolutely himself, despite the dementia.

IN THE EVENING, WE'LL DANCE

≈

Our friend Loree told me that many aspects of her father's essential self remained throughout his decline from dementia—even though he was challenged by hallucinations and an inability to speak clearly. He could perceive the world around him but couldn't articulate his perceptions. It was, she said, as if "a thick veil" hung upon him. I imagine him straining under the weight of that pall as it clung to him, like a shirt of chainmail. He may have felt as one does when struggling to surface from a nightmare: limbs too heavy, tongue too thick. Unable to move. Unable to call out.

Loree's voice and touch reassured her father; he was comforted by her presence. Lacking those connections, she believes he may have retreated behind his mantle and collapsed into himself.

She didn't back away due to fears of dementia. Rather, Loree persisted in reaching out for her father, knowing that "the two of us could still truly find each other." She could find him because she expected him to be there.

The scholar Gisela Webb had similar experiences with her mother, who was dying of Alzheimer's. Those moments gave Webb "the impression, and I must say certitude, that there is an essential knowing self, the soul, somewhat trapped beneath the veils of the decaying mind/brain and body."

Both women continued to seek out the essential selves of their loved ones.

≈

In 2005, the year that his dementia worsened markedly, Dick wrote *Dick Cain, Tracer of Lost Persons* on a scrap of notepaper, then drew a descending series of spiraling lines beneath it.

A snippet from his childhood had shown up, like a tattered ticket falling from an opened book. When he was a boy in Minneapolis, he'd enjoyed radio shows. He told me that he'd preferred mysteries. He may well have listened to a detective show called *Mr. Keen, Tracer of Lost Persons*. It aired for almost two decades, beginning in 1937; Dick would have been five years old then.

Unlike Sherlock Holmes' logical reasoning, Mr. Keen had "hunches" that came over him and helped him solve crimes. Most of the scripts required the elderly sleuth to solve murder mysteries, notes Jim Cox in his history of the show. However, the theme song, "Someday I'll Find You," featured the idea of locating a missing person. In the script for the first episode on October 12, 1937, the show is described as "the story of a man [Mr. Keen] who believes everyone in the world has lost someone they'd like to find again."

The someone whom Dick sought to find was himself. It was as if he had become a character in the episode entitled "The Case of the Man in Search of Himself." Mr. Cain/Mr. Keen christened himself a "tracer of lost persons" during the most bewildering period of his dementia. The word *trace* is from an Old French word, *tracier*, which means to make one's way by searching. Dick Cain was both the tracer of lost persons and the person who was lost.

One of the first signs of dementia is losing the ability to navigate. The person can no longer trace his mental maps. He gets lost. Much of the world around him becomes perilous, uncharted territory.

Dick had been a man who knew his way in the world. That world grew more circumscribed as his dementia progressed. At first, he still knew his way to the town south of our log house. When he could no longer drive, Dick found his way back home while riding his bike, confined by the script of a half-mile gravel road. Eventually, a small, secure center—our neighborhood, our home, me—demarcated Dick's world.

Overwhelmed by his disease, Dick retreated from a frightening unknown to the security of the known. His inner atlas placed "order at the center and wilderness and chaos at the edges," like the ancient maps that "mirrored the psyche," as the writer Amelia Soth puts it.

≈

When Dick neared the late stages of dementia, I'd hover over him while he sat on the toilet. (To tell you this seems like an affront to my husband's dignity, but it's a reality of caregiving.) I'd remind him, "Wipe your butt carefully."

"I know that!" he retorted. "*I'm my own person.*" Every word of that sentence refers to selfhood:

I	Refers to oneself as speaker or writer. The self. The ego. It's a nominative pronoun, meaning it's the subject of the verb—in this case, *am.*
Am	First personal singular of *to be*, to exist; to have life or reality.
My	Possessive form of *I.* Of or relating to ownership or possession.
Own	That which belongs to oneself.
Person	An individual human being. Traditionally thought of as consisting of both a body and a mind or soul.

Within the first week of my moving Dick to an assisted living facility, an aide informed me that he, insulted, had told her, "I'm not a child!" He also exclaimed to me, "I'm a human being!" Dick insisted on living in accord with his character and his own wishes.

Dick Cain was a person first, a human being who happened to have dementia. He continued to be "shaped around 'I' like a flame on a wick, emanating itself in grief and guilt and joy," as the narrator Rev. John Ames says of his parishioners, in Marilynne Robinson's novel *Gilead.*

≈

What does it mean to *have* a self, as if it's a possession? An acquaintance told me this story: She was at the nursing home visiting her mother-in-law, who had dementia. They joined another resident for coffee. Her mother-in-law looked at her and said, "You have a self." Then she turned to the other resident and said, "You have a self."

"What about you?" asked her daughter-in-law.

"But I, I . . ." was the reply.

Due to her dementia, the woman had lost most of her memories.

It's likely that she'd also lost her home and many of her belongings when she moved to the nursing home. The facility's maze of long hallways and sundry rooms probably baffled her. I imagine that she often felt lost.

Perhaps she hesitated because she couldn't explain to her guests that, despite those losses, she was still there—just not quite the person she once was. Even so, she still possessed an *I*.

This is most often the case. Persons with advanced dementia continue to use the first person "I" frequently and coherently in reference to themselves, their needs, and their concerns. Their use of the personal pronouns, *I, me, mine, myself*, persists and serves as a "representation of self," as the psychologist Steven Sabat observes.

"I like feeling you," said Dick as I rubbed his chest. "No. That's not right! You're feeling me. We need to keep track of who's who." To whom do *I* and *me* refer, if not the self?

≈

Rather than *having* a self, perhaps one could consider what it means to *be* a self. I rummaged through numerous philosophical and neurological theories, in search of the elusive idea of "self." Finally, I found a conception that fit my own experience with my husband's dementia. Throughout his decline, Dick remained sentient, an embodied being in the world—his brain, body, emotions, other people, and the world of the senses all intertwined.

The idea of the self as thus intertwined runs counter to the prevailing notion that we *are* our brains; many consider the brain to be the "seat of our identity." This brain-centric position, which some researchers object to as being "hyper-cognitive" or "neuro-reductionist," results in the privileging of rationality, intellect, and memory. It colors our view of persons with dementia.

"We owe it to those who have aging brains not to reduce their humanity to one organ," asserts Peter Whitehouse, a neurologist. The biophysicist Alan Jasanoff also argues against such brain-centrism, labeling it "the cerebral mystique." He notes that the brain "never works alone." Our brains function in contexts, in relationship with internal and external forces. The brain is "inextricably linked" to the rest of the body and the environment around it. The environment floods the brain with sensory input. Some of those stimuli, such as winter's low light or a clap of thunder, subconsciously influence our emotions and moods.

Jasanoff also points out that "signals from within the body influence behaviors just as powerfully as influences from the environment." He cites the fight-or-flight response as illustrative of this complex brain-body circuitry: fear-related signals from the brain's hypothalamus trigger glands atop our kidneys to secrete hormones, causing our hearts to race and heightening our sensory acuity. Working in concert, body and brain ready us to either fight or flee.

And what of people whose brains have been compromised? Even in those with severe cognitive disability, many neurons continue to function; people in the later stages of the disease are still conscious. Dr. Michael Gazzaniga, a neuroscientist, explains that consciousness is resilient and observes, "There are consciousnesses all over the brain." Even in persons with dementia, areas of the brain remain intact. Information still is processed in those undamaged areas and will "induce a subjective feeling of experience. The contents of that conscious experience may be very different from normal, but consciousness remains." The dialogue between self and world continues, although the nature of that exchange may have altered dramatically.

When Dick resided in an assisted living home, I visited him daily and observed residents' reactions to others and to their environment. They'd express their anger, affection, frustration, delight, and sadness. Even if they'd lost language, they'd not lost affective ways of knowing. And they usually could make their feelings known.

I heard the sleepy lounge spring alive with singing and rhythmic clapping when musicians played. I saw a woman with impaired speech crook her index finger, motioning to me to "come here." When I leaned down to her in the wheelchair, she smiled and kissed me on the cheek. I heard the strident shrieks of another woman whenever the aides took her to the shower room. She did *not* want her clothing removed by a stranger. She didn't say as much; she didn't have to.

In persons with dementia, "the life of the emotions is often intense," although they may struggle to understand their feelings, notes the psychologist Tom Kitwood. They also are "more in tune with the body and its functions, closer to the life of instinct." Since we live in such a hyper-cognitive culture, Kitwood suggests that people with dementia "may have something important to teach the rest of humankind" about integrating mind and body.

≈

When I was a child, an old woman lived near my grandmother's home. My sister and I never saw her. We saw her rotting house, shrouded with shrubs and vines, shades drawn. A witch's house! In a thrill of fear, we'd run past the place. We wondered what might lurk inside, peering out at us as we ran.

That fear of the unknown resembles the way some respond to people with dementia. Do they fear what resides inside? Or do they fear that seeming vacancy?

What if we were to seek for the person inside, rather than running away? What if we would pause long enough to "notice an enduring self" and perceive the "mind behind the mind," wonders Stephen G. Post, a medical ethicist. I think Post is referring to the essence of a person. Some refer to it as the psyche or the soul. Whether or not one is religious, *soul* is "a useful construct," notes Nina Strohminger, an ethicist. It signifies the fundamental nature of a person, an immaterial, but essential, core.

People who work closely with or live with individuals who have dementia often recognize this and will declare that she or he is still "in there." When he was young, the bioethicist Jesse Ballenger worked as a nursing assistant. He observed that the personal self persists, even in persons with severe dementia. They "had an identity and an independent will that had to be reckoned with."

Although someone with dementia undergoes many changes, family members often don't think that they've become a different person. In a 2015 study published in *Psychological Science*, close relatives were asked, "How much do you sense that the patient is still the same person underneath?" Most continued to see their loved one as the person he or she had always been—regardless of the severity of the dementia. They'd agree with the psychologist Michael Bender, who argues, "I-ness is resistant to cognitive losses."

That I-ness, that essence, that "DickCainness" of my husband, remained to the end.

≈

At a dinner party with friends, I said that I was writing this essay. My central assertion, I explained, was that the self persists in people with dementia. As I spoke, our hostess looked down, worrying the food on her plate.

Then I mentioned an intriguing study I'd recently read. The researchers, philosophers Nina Strohminger and Shaun Nichols, identified retention of the moral faculty—rather than retention of memory—as key to the persistence of identity in people with dementia. They included traits such as compassion, empathy, and honesty in their definition of moral character. They'd interviewed family members of people with two types of dementia: Alzheimer's and frontotemporal (FT). Most families thought their loved ones with Alzheimer's remained fundamentally the same. However, this wasn't the case with FT dementia. Damage in the frontal areas of the brain can affect what's referred to as "executive functions," blunting compassion and lowering inhibitions. This can result in a dramatic change in behavior and in moral traits.

The hostess looked up at me: "I'm so relieved to hear you say that." Her mother, she told me, had not seemed like the same woman at all after she got dementia—but it was frontotemporal.

Dick did not have FT dementia. He remained himself in many ways, but his experience of the world around him was harrowing at times, as he battled demons during the middle stages of the disease. That's when he knew something was drastically wrong, but he couldn't remember what it was. And due to his cognitive losses, he couldn't understand it. He fought against his fear with ferocity and, at times, physical violence.

During that turbulent period, I worried that he'd lost his moral center. I feared that the gentle, kind man I'd always known may have vanished. If he had died then, it would have left me even more bereft.

But Dick's experience of the world shifted again during his later years, to one that was generally benign. It's not uncommon for calm to follow the storms of the middle phase in persons with dementia. Perhaps their further cognitive losses render them unable to continue the battle, or they are too weak physically, or they have arrived at acceptance.

To my relief, my husband's moral self was intact. He continued to have empathy for others, manifested in his strong, vocal commitment to equal rights and social justice. Although he no longer knew what day, month, or year it was, when the Minnesota Lynx won the 2011 women's national basketball championship, Dick said, "Good. I'm for equality for women." After viewing a news report about discrimination against Black Americans, he'd exclaimed, "That's not right!"

≈

The words we often use to describe people with dementia can blind us to the self that remains. The bioethicist Stephen G. Post asks, "Why do we hear metaphors such as *absent, gone, husk, dead, empty*, and the like?" Post's list of metaphors is not encompassing. In addition to "absent, gone, husks, dead, empty," consider images such as a *vegetable, shell, ghost*. It's as if the body serves solely as a container for the mind, which the person supposedly has *lost*. There's *no one home*.

Many more such metaphors appear in both popular and scholarly articles. In a recent book on dementia (2018), Steven R. Sabat states that "even among professionals, horrifically negative stereotypes exist regarding persons with dementia."

Dementia is described as

an *abyss*,

a *world of doom*,

a *fate worse than death*,

a *mind-robber*,

an *erasure of selfhood*,

an *unbecoming,*
a *living death,*
a *life not worth living.*

A person with dementia is
not there,
a *blank,*
a *shadow,*
a *walking corpse,*
a *zombie.*

The self supposedly
is *slowly eaten alive,*
disintegrates,
is *dismantled,*
until there's *nothing left.*

The person becomes a *nonperson*
who has *disappeared.*

≈

How can one describe dementia, a disease that seems unfathomable? In our devastation and dread, we struggle to find the words. We may grasp at the metaphors we've read or heard. Or perhaps we choose such words in order to close off our fears, to create distance between *them* (those with dementia) and *us* ("normal").

The Nazis labeled people with dementia as *untermenschen,* subhuman. They portrayed them as burdens to society, as "useless eaters," as "life unworthy of life." If they remained in an institution, they were starved or killed by lethal injection. Many were carted off to gas chambers in buses, the windows painted over so people couldn't see the victims inside. Local children called the buses "killing crates." The Nazis murdered more than 200,000 mentally and physically handicapped people, according to the U.S. Holocaust Memorial Museum.

Now, almost eight decades after the Nazi's euthanasia program, some utilitarian philosophers have argued that people with dementia are "non-person humans" and killing them may be justified. This position, articulated by the contemporary philosopher Peter Singer, is extreme. He argues that society shouldn't use its limited resources on people who have lost their utility. They should be euthanized because "the person we knew is gone," Singer wrote in a 2014 article.

However, when his own mother developed Alzheimer's, Singer and his sister elected to pay for her care, even though their mother had requested that she not be cared for if she was no longer useful in her old age. Singer explained to the journalist Michael Specter, "Perhaps it is more difficult than I thought before, because it is different when it's your mother."

By stigmatizing people with dementia—viewing them as diseased outcasts, as "non-persons"—it becomes easier to rationalize a lack of care for that person.

≈

Infants cannot speak. Some people who have dementia no longer can speak. Caregivers feed and clothe infants and change their diapers. These are the same types of care given to those in the late stages of dementia. Yet we view infants as delightful beings. We interact with them—cooing, singing, laughing, talking, touching, playing. We try to read their every expression, gesture, and cry. Why, then, the sudden illiteracy when faced with a person who has dementia? If we've written them off as "not there," a blank page, then any attempt to read them probably seems pointless.

We embrace infants as persons, yet some view those with dementia as non-persons. Why? Perhaps because infants are nascent buds about to bloom, while the elderly are waning. We sense the infants' promise, whereas the aged have reached fruition.

Our lives are bounded at either end: by the mysteries of beginnings as well as of endings, of births as well as of deaths. An infant arrives in the world. An elder nears the terminus. Terminus was the god who presided over boundaries in ancient Rome. The Romans honored him. As should we.

≈

And what of me? Have I always honored those with dementia? How do I plead?

Guilty: A hulking man hovered over Mother and me as we sat together in the nursing home's dining room. I tried to ignore him as I read to her from our hometown newspaper. He stared at us and gestured; he was no longer able to speak. I wanted him to go away. His silence, his presence, felt menacing. It unnerved me. I realized that he, like my late husband, probably had dementia. But it didn't matter. I didn't want this cipher looming over us.

Mother, who was kinder than I, said, "I think he wants to look at the paper." She handed it to him. His eyes skimmed the newsprint sheet, clotted with words. He could no longer read them. He set down the paper and lumbered away. "Good riddance," I thought.

Guilty: I wanted to silence Emily's tremulous, high-pitched pleas. They emanated from behind a curtain that divided the room my mother shared with her in the nursing home. Over and over, Emily would call out, "Pleeeeease. Pleeeeeeease. Help me!" I'd draw back the curtain and ask her, "What's wrong, Emily? How can I help you?" A look of confusion would cross her face, and she'd grow silent. I'd close the curtain and return to Mother's bedside. "Pleeeeease. Pleeeeeeease. Help me!"

Guilty: I wanted to be rid of the man who repeatedly called out "HELP ME! HELP ME! HELP ME!" His cries carried down the hallway to Dick's room in a geriatric psychiatric unit. It distressed him. He wrote a note to me about "the man who's yelling 'Help.'" He talked to the nurses about it. They told him that there was nothing they could do.

The crying man lay in a darkened room, his mattress on the floor. That much I saw. Then I looked away; I wanted to shut him out. I wanted to shut him up.

Guilty: In 2008—after Dick and I had lived through ten years of his decline—I learned from a Mayo Clinic neurologist that my husband probably was near the middle of the disease process. He could live another ten years. Or more. I railed against this news: "That's the rest of *my* life!" After that, sometimes I'd place my hand on my husband's chest to feel its subtle rise and fall, hoping that he was – wasn't / was – wasn't / was – wasn't / was still alive.

I struggled for years, blinkered by my battle against his disease. I read pamphlets that described the signs of dementia, ticking off his losses. The list lengthened. Dementia was relentless. Dementia was merciless.

Finally, I called a truce with dementia. Dementia simply *was*—a reality we both had to accept.

≈

Determined that Dick and I would continue to find one another, I sought out places where we might meet. Some people join with their loved ones in prayers or songs. Some may watch a ball game or a sunset together. Others may simply fold laundry, side-by-side. Dick and I continued to share a textured life, interwoven with music, language, flavors, and touch.

I'd envelop him in nets of words, of music—jazz and classical music, mainly—and of color. On the wall opposite his bed, I hung a large, whimsical painting of a medieval cityscape with flag-topped towers and arched doorways. I decorated other walls with some van Gogh prints and Dick's photos from Granada and Toledo.

Above his bed, I placed a framed Rumi quotation: "Wherever you stand, be the soul of that place." I wanted Dick to remain standing in that place. To remain standing in his own person, despite the dementia. And he did.

CHAPTER 10

Jenny, Anna, Joe

Dick made a valiant effort not to forget. Regularly, and always in the same order, he would repeat: *Jenny, Anna, Joe, Calvin, Doris, Stephanie, Alden, Jim, Rosie, Grace, and Ashlyn*. He learned his list of family names by heart.

To "learn by heart" may come from the Old Testament. When Solomon imparts his words of wisdom, he urges his listeners to "write them upon the tablet of your heart." With each iteration, Dick engraved the names more deeply.

I entered his list in my commonplace book, with a note that I thought it was important—even urgent—to write it down then, in June of 2011. I didn't know how much longer he'd be able to recite their names. He remembered the list for two more years. By 2013, two years before his death, it was gone.

He began with the most important names, those of his children, Jenny, Anna, and Joe. He also included their spouses (Jim, Alden, Stephanie), his grandchildren (Calvin, Grace, Ashlyn), his deceased aunt (Doris), and, for some reason, Jenny's dead dog (Rosie).

His efforts to remember moved me. Perhaps that's why, over the many years of his recitation, I never wondered about the missing names. I do now. Where were his parents? Where was his first wife, Ruth, the mother of Jenny, Anna, and Joe? Where was I?

≈

I'd taken a photo of Dick with his grandson during Calvin's graduation party in 2006. Their heads are cocked toward one another, Dick's arm around Calvin's shoulders. The resemblance is clear in the face shapes, prominent noses, and wry smiles—but not their eyes. Calvin's dark eyes shine; Dick's appear vague, veiled. A lowered brow shrouds his left eye.

It was 99 degrees and sunny. Calvin's high school friends slammed the screen door as they wandered in and out of the house. Listless family members gathered in the back yard. They'd circled chairs under pools of shade cast by a few trees.

Dick and I greeted Jenny, Anna, Joe, and their families. By then, he often could not recall acquaintances' names, but he usually remembered the names of friends—and always of family. We stopped to greet his former wife, Ruth. Dick hesitated. The silence lengthened. Within that pause, a new lapse was laid bare: he didn't recognize Ruth, his wife of fifteen years.

She was calm and gracious. She smiled up at him: "Hello, Dick. I'm Ruth."

≈

Dick always began his recitation with the names of his children in their birth order. I believe it was his way of declaring himself "Father of Jenny, Anna, and Joe." His assertion reminds me of the Biblical *begats*—which, in newer translations, has evolved into "became the father of."

Dick's fatherhood resembled an inner map on which he could always locate himself, like a genealogist tracing branches in a family tree. Genealogy places a person within a larger story, and it provides an answer to the question, "Who are you?" Dick knew who he was when he declared his fatherhood.

Not that he always recognized his kids. He often would confuse Jenny with Anna. Once, he greeted Joe and his wife Stephanie with the names of our close friends Stan and Susan. But when reminded of who they were, he would relax. He still sensed that his son and daughters were part of him.

Pia Kontos, a medical anthropologist, argues that people with dementia retain certain kinds of knowing. It's knowledge that's embodied; it "resides below the threshold of cognition." For example, Willem de Kooning continued to paint even as his Alzheimer's advanced. The spare works from this late period seem to be, as one critic observes, created by "following his hand." Despite his dementia, what de Kooning saw still could be expressed through the gesture of brush on canvas, through embodied know-how.

Familial recognition is a kind of embodied knowing. The father of our friend Doug had advanced dementia. Doug told me that, during a visit, his father "started talking to me as if I were a stranger," addressing his son with surprise: "How interesting! So you attended Cornell, too." And yet he was at ease with his son in a way he wouldn't have been with a stranger. Doug's father recognized him at some other, deeper, level.

Re-cognition means "to know again." We often define cognition narrowly, as mentation. But there are other ways of acquiring knowledge: through sensation, perception, and intuition. The parent-child relationship is encoded in the muscles that cradled the infant, the nerves that responded to every cry. This love is "rooted not in the mind but in the heart and will thus persist even when [the] dementia advances," observes Kontos.

≈

Is a vague familial recognition enough? How does it feel to have your name lost to a parent who named and nurtured you?

Several years ago, when Jenny, Anna, and Joe were all in their early fifties, I asked them to choose a few adjectives to describe their dad prior to his dementia. He was, they said, *witty, funny, smart, strong, able, handsome, caring, loving, understanding,* and "passionate about life and the things that he believed in." Just as I'd seen him.

As Dick lived through the late stages of dementia, he—and they—lost much of what made him the father he had been. Where was that able, strong man? They still loved him, but, as one of them said, "He does not feel like my dad." A friend found that statement shocking. I didn't.

They felt a mixture of sadness, anger, impatience, and guilt. So did I. He was still funny at times, but they also described him as *repetitive, tedious, scared*—and *scary*. Sometimes, they said, they feared him, because he could be angry or unpredictable. He seemed distant. He was "not himself." The picture they had of their father—and he of them—had grown distorted.

≈

We scan a face, moving from the eyes, to the nose, to the mouth—back and forth, gathering it in. We trace its particular geography with our eyes, memorizing the face and attaching a name to it. To call someone by name is to designate her, to distinguish her from others. Until her name is recalled, she remains anonymous.

When I was young, I wondered what *Anon*, the abbreviation for anonymous, meant. Since it was capitalized, I assumed it was a proper name. Based on this supposition, I developed a fanciful misconception. I noticed *Anon* at the end of a few poems and imagined the poet *Anon* as a tragic figure who wrote a few verses and died young. I visualized her drowned and drifting, like Ophelia.

As long as a person remains nameless, it's as if she is submerged, obscured by turbid waters. We all have had such moments. You're at a party or cafe or grocery store when you see someone you know you know. She greets you: "Hello! How nice to see you again." You can't recall her name. It discomfits you.

I imagine Dick diving down, in hopes of retrieving the mislaid name. "Who is she? Who?" whirring in his mind beneath the idle chit-chat. Nothing. She remained nameless—nameless to a man who valued language, naming, and names.

Dick resided in an assisted living home during the final two years of his life. While visiting with him one evening, I observed the importance he still placed on names. We were seated in the commons area when an aide spoke to another resident, addressing her as "little lady." Dick was clearly irritated: "What's her name? Call her by her name!"

Then he spoke his own name, "Richard Ralph Cain."

IN THE EVENING, WE'LL DANCE

≈

First, he lost the names. Then the memory of some faces was lost to him, as well. Those faces he had so carefully mapped in his mind began to recede. In a way, it was as if he became blind to them.

A few people, perfectly normal in every other respect, have a condition called face blindness. Its scientific name, *prosopagnosia*, derives from the Greek words for *face* and *not knowing*. A face doesn't convey identity to individuals who do not "know faces." Loved ones may look no different than strangers; a mother may not recognize her own daughter. Every face is a puzzle to them. They perceive parts—hair, mouth, eyes—but those parts don't converge to make a unified whole, or gestalt. They may single out one piece of that puzzle, one feature, as an identity clue. The neurologist Oliver Sacks could not recognize his own face in a mirror, so he singled out a feature, his large ears, as a way to recognize himself.

Dementia also can affect visual face perception. A 2016 study by Canadian researchers, led by neuropsychologist Sven Joubert, revealed that holistic perception—the ability to see another's face as a whole, rather than the discrete parts (eyes, nose, mouth)—is impaired in people with dementia.

One young woman who developed face blindness following an accident describes it as "struggling to find a connection," as if she's "lost everybody." She desperately wants, she says, "to find a branch that will just pull everybody back."

The branch Dick clung to for many years was his list of names.

≈

In many folktales, calling out a name gives the protagonist control over a giant, troll, werewolf, or demon. Probably the most well-known example of this is "Rumpelstiltskin," the tale of a dwarf who spins straw into gold for a young maid. In exchange, he demands her firstborn. When she bears a child, the dwarf says he'll relent if the maid guesses his name. She does. The infant is spared and Rumpelstiltskin, enraged that his name has been revealed, tears himself in half.

83

Pre-literate peoples believed in the power of the name; to utter a name gave the speaker mastery. By learning a person's name, an enemy could gain control over him or her, perhaps by casting an evil spell. Some believed that they could abscond with a person's soul by writing down his or her name. Many cultures still prohibit speaking the deceased's name for fear of evoking the ghost.

Thus, people have developed taboos about revealing names, whether they be of individuals or sacred beings. Due to this prohibition, in some cultures, people use a known, or public, name, sometimes called the "little name." They also have a secret "great" or "true" name.

The creation story told in Genesis also clearly connects naming and power. God names a thing and it comes into being: "God said, 'Let there be Light' and there was light." When God created man, he charged him with naming the animals in the Garden of Eden.

≈

Ever since Adam, humans seem compelled to name things—the earth's flora and fauna, subatomic particles, celestial phenomena, cloud formations and winds, the vagaries of the weather, and our own inner weathers and workings.

Explorers and scientists label geographic places and landforms, the matter, minutiae, and mechanics of the heavens and the earth. Even in Death Valley, the hottest place on earth, humans paused to bestow place names: Badwater Basin, Furnace Creek, Hell's Gate.

The only opportunity most people have to name something is when they decide what to call their children. It's a momentous choice, conferring the name a person will bear throughout a lifetime. Dick and Ruth turned to song, sound, and heritage when naming their children. Jenny, their first-born, was named after a favorite Leadbelly song, "Sweet Jenny Lee." They called their middle child *Anna Rachel* and their youngest *Joseph,* because they liked the way those names sounded. The name of Ruth's paternal grandfather, *Alexander*, was bestowed on Joe as his middle name.

IN THE EVENING, WE'LL DANCE

≈

When Dick was seventy-four, he was evaluated at the Mayo Clinic in Rochester. The discharge summary described him as "pleasantly confused." His thought process was "vague," and the doctors discerned "limited judgment and insight." His diagnosis: *dementia, probable Alzheimer's type.*

I asked his physician if that meant he would wander about, a lost soul, like a few of the patients I'd seen. It was likely, yes.

I asked if that meant someday he would no longer know my name, know who I am. Again, that was probable. I said I'd rather one of us would die before it would come to that. How could I become a stranger to the man I'd loved for decades?

So every night at bedtime, we'd kiss and then I'd say, "I love you, Dick Cain."

He'd smile and reply, "I love you, Anne-Marie Erickson."

Even as he neared the end of his life, my name and voice would call him up from deep slumbers when aides were unable to. He'd lie motionless, eyelids closed tightly against any efforts to rouse him. I'd call his name; his lids would flutter, and he'd warily peek through his lashes. "Annie?"

I'd answer, "Yes, it's me, Annie." Then Dick would open his eyes and re-enter the world.

At the end of the visit, I'd kiss him and say, "I love you, Dick Cain."

Often, there was a pause. Then, "And I love *you*, Anne-Marie Erickson."

≈

Many of us learned a little verse set to music called the "ABC" song when we were children. Like other nursery rhymes, the tune employs rhythm and rhyme, which serve as mnemonic devices, or memory aids. The simple ditty helps children learn the alphabet by rote, as they sing it over and over. Learning by rote requires repetition—of nursery rhymes or keyboard scales or verb conjugations—until they "stick." Dick's regular repetition of his list of names was a kind of rote learning, and it stuck for many years.

Much of our human heritage—whether it be Homeric epics, the poetry of the Gaelic bards, Native American lore, or Icelandic sagas—initially was preserved in oral form, repeatedly spoken, sung, or chanted. Dick's recitation of names resembled an incantation, a chant that has the magic power to keep memories alive. He spoke the names slowly, always with the same tempo and rhythm.

≈

Physical objects also can serve as markers and memory cues. The beads in a rosary, for example, are used to recall and count a sequence of prayers. In West Africa, specific stories might be represented by objects strung from a cord, such as feathers and stones.

Stones serve as a means to mark the way home in the "Hansel and Gretel" fairy tale. When the children overhear their stepmother plotting to abandon them deep in the forest, Hansel concocts a plan. After their father and stepmother fall asleep, Hansel slips outdoors and picks up small stones, stowing them in his pockets.

The next day they follow their parents into the woods. Hansel drops the pebbles behind him. When night falls, the parents abandon the children in the depths of the woods. A full moon rises and shines down on the pebbles so they glow "like silver coins." Hansel and Gretel walk through the night; the trail of pebbles leads them home.

Like Hansel, Dick dropped pebbles—*Jenny, Anna, Joe, Calvin, Doris, Stephanie, Alden, Jim, Rosie, Grace, Ashlyn*—to mark his way home.

CHAPTER 11

Yesterday I Knew Who That Was

Dementia, that thief, moved into our lives in 1998. It picked the pockets of my husband's mind: first, the front pockets that held his recent memories, then the back pockets, with the older memories. It stole the names of friends, then the names of his children, *Jenny, Anna,* and *Joe*. And, sometimes, my name: *Who are you? Susan? Kate?*

≈

Just as we'd fought off a pair of Roma pickpockets in Madrid, we struggled desperately against this thief. We wrestled with the confusion, fear, and anger that arose with each new loss. At times, we fought against one another.

I documented it all—the lapses, the losses, the battles. I chronicled his medical appointments, late-night trips to the emergency room, the many hospitalizations. I made note of the drugs that failed, the few drugs that helped. I stowed it all: his agenda books, my letters and e-mail messages to family and friends, my jottings on scraps of paper and in commonplace books.

I've used commonplace books for years. They function as repositories for my observations, quotations from my reading, poems, witticisms, and an occasional sketch of a flower or bird. My book from 2010-2014 contains quotations from a lecture I attended on resilience, from Alfred Kazin's essay on the art of the memoir, and from a memoir about loss by Joan Didion.

More than half of the pages in that commonplace book hold my notes—usually dated, often barely legible—of what Dick had said: *D. said. D. commented. D. sang.* To be a scribe, capturing his words, was a way of doing battle with the thief.

But these words are mine: *My husband has dementia.* How many times had I said those words over the decade before his death? And in the seven years prior to an official diagnosis, how often had I avoided saying them, or even thinking them?

Now, I want to parse that phrase. To parse a sentence is to pull it apart, scrutinizing each word. One can even create something called a parse tree, a diagram of the sentence parts. A parse tree sounds lovely, even festive.

When I was in eighth grade, the parsing seemed barbarous, a poor sentence sprawled on the blackboard, swatted down and flattened out. Our grammar teacher, Miss Mangan, diagramed sentences with a fierceness that made the fat on her upper arms jiggle. No pretty parse trees, just broken chalk and frightened kids.

Then I became the English teacher. I told my freshman composition students that the heart of a sentence consists of an *actor* (the subject) and an *action* (the predicate). I'd write a basic sentence on the board: *I* (actor) *sing* (action).

"That's a sentence? Two words?" they'd exclaim.

"They should know this," I thought, but many of them looked mystified, perhaps because I'd mentioned *grammar* and *heart* in the same sentence.

I also told my students that as I'd diagramed Miss Mangan's sentences so many years ago, I realized how the pieces, the words and phrases, could be moved about. It gave me a sense of control over them.

My husband has dementia. How can I wrest control over such a sentence?

My

My is a possessive. It tells the reader whose husband is under consideration. Notice that I'm not using the other possible possessive, *Her* husband. Or an article, such as *The* husband or *A* husband. It would make it easier if I could hold the sentence at arm's length. But there's no escaping the fact that he was *my* beloved for more than forty-two years.

husband

The subject of my sentence is *husband*. The word derives from the Old Norse, *húsbóndi*. *Hús* means *house,* and *bondi* can be translated as "tiller of the soil." Many of our short and earthy words come from the Old Norse, such as *cut, dirt, root, house*, and *till.*

The *húsbóndi* domesticates the land. He puts down roots. The word bears layers of meaning that capture, in many ways, who Dick was when I met him. He'd put down roots, living in an old farmhouse on a half-acre of land in White Bear Lake, Minnesota. He was the father of three children. And he was a gardener.

≈

I was twenty-four when I decided that I wanted to be a tiller of the soil. Most of the time, I'd felt as if I were two feet above the ground. A Yiddish word best describes my youthful self: *Luftmensch*, a dreamer, an "air person." It was time I planted myself.

I lived in Minneapolis, on the West Bank of the Mississippi River. North Country Co-op, the first natural foods grocery in the city, was across the street from my rooms in a tumbledown duplex. The produce displays drew me in—bright greens, reds, and yellows, like the bold colors in the *Dick and Jane* basic readers from my childhood. As I breathed in the loamy aromas, I yearned for a plot of earth. I wanted to grow my own vegetables.

Then I met a man who was a gardener. I told him that I'd been yearning to have a garden of my own.

≈

Eventually, Dick no longer could run the line of twine to delineate a row, nor etch trenches for plump bean seeds, nor sow them. I'd dig, weed, and cultivate. I'd pluck pea pods and ripe tomatoes from their vines. He would sit in the shade and watch me work. Each spring my husband would ask, "Will we have a garden?"

He still gardens with me, even after his death. His is the voice that I hear in my mind: "Be patient. There's no point in planting until the soil is warm." "Pinch back those suckers on the tomato plants." "Wait until dusk to water."

has

When a person suffers from an illness, we use the verb *has*: he has the flu, she has the measles. In this sense, Dick *had* dementia. But did he have dementia, or did dementia have him?

dementia

I use the noun *dementia* to describe my husband's decline. Beneath that umbrella term several specific neurocognitive disorders huddle, including Alzheimer's, Lewy body, frontotemporal, and vascular dementias. All of the dementias involve damage to the brain that leads to a decline in cognitive abilities, such as memory, judgment, comprehension, logic, and language.

Ultimately, his physicians at Mayo Clinic thought Dick might have a "mixed dementia" that combined Alzheimer's with vascular and Lewy body dementias. Persons with Alzheimer's have memory problems and gradually experience difficulties with language, organization, and everyday tasks. Lewy body manifests with visual hallucinations early in the disease and affects reasoning and problem solving. A person may act out his or her dreams, which is something Dick did intermittently throughout his decline. He would kick, swing his arms, and flail about as he played tennis or fought off an intruder in his dreams.

Vascular dementia may be the result of a stroke. It also can be caused by conditions such as the high blood pressure Dick had, which can damage blood vessels and reduce circulation. Symptoms will vary, depending on which part of the brain is deprived of blood flow. They may include Alzheimer's-like symptoms, as well as problems with balance, walking, and gait. Confusion and trouble with concentration also occur. Changes happen suddenly, then plateau, in a step-like fashion, in contrast to the steady downward slope of Alzheimer's.

Fortunately, Dick didn't have one of the most disturbing forms of dementia: frontotemporal. It causes extreme changes in a person's personality and behavior, as well as difficulties with or loss of language. As the name implies, it primarily impacts the frontal and temporal lobes of the brain, whereas Alzheimer's affects most of the brain. Frontotemporal tends to occur earlier in life than the other dementias, from ages forty to sixty-five.

≈

The literal meaning of *dement* is "to lose mentation or the ability to think." It derives from the Latin *demens*, which means "out of one's mind." Dick was not out of his mind. He was not *deranged, crazed, lunatic, unhinged, psycho, nutty, batty, loopy, loony, bonkers,* or *wacko*—all synonyms for *demented.* He was a person who had dementia, not a demented person. His disease didn't define him.

My husband's neurons were damaged. Doctors call it "atrophy of the brain." He was, as some experts say, "deeply forgetful." Although he'd lost most of his memories, Dick retained an in-the-moment awareness of his perceptions, his feelings, and the beauties of this world. At times, he was surprisingly lucid. Sometimes he was witty. And sometimes he was quite wise.

Nonetheless, aspects of my husband were no longer present. They'd faded away. Near the end of his life, I showed him a photo of the two of us and asked him, "Do you know who these people are?" He looked closely, then drew back.

"Yesterday I knew who that was," he replied.

•

Period. End of sentence. But this sentence, *My husband has dementia,* often ends up defining the spouse, too.

PART 3

Battered, Not Broken

CHAPTER 12

Who Are You?

Quite often during the last years of my husband's life, people would ask me, "Does Dick still know who you are?"

What if he didn't? What if my answer were "No"? It's a rather cruel question, if you think about it. Imagine greeting an acquaintance in the store aisle, leaning on your grocery cart, tinny Muzak sifting down as you tell a person this: My beloved husband doesn't know who I am.

The question would rip into me. I'd collect myself. I'd tell them something true: "There have been times when he hasn't known who I am. But he almost always recognizes me and calls me by name."

There. I'd expertly executed yet another pivot. When people asked me how my husband was, I often would pivot on the hinge of a *but*: "We had a rough morning—but then he sang to me and told me that he loves me."

I was truthful, to a point. This is what I'd leave unsaid: "He usually knows me. But on those few occasions when he doesn't? I'm alarmed. Angry. Devastated."

One of the painful mysteries behind dementia is that often the person with the disease knows and then does not; the loved one is known, then is not. But I was known. Until his death, my husband usually greeted me delightedly. Every time he did this, it gave me so much joy. On those few occasions when he didn't seem to recognize me and couldn't recall my name, it was as if he'd slapped me.

Even in those moments, I believe that he retained a felt sense that we belonged to one another. The confounding answer to the question "Does he still know you?" would have to be both yes and no. In the final year of Dick's life, I showed him a photo of Jenny, his eldest child.

I asked him, "Who is this?" He didn't say her name. Rather, he replied, "She's near to me." He didn't know her, and yet he did.

≈

Commentary: Once Dick said to me, "I know you and I love you." At the time, I thought it significant that he chose to say, "I know you."

2010

It started in August. Dick would sometimes ask me, "Who are you?"

On a hot afternoon, he rested on the couch and I on the recliner. Suddenly, he opened his eyes and asked, "Are you Paula? Joyce?"—the names of two of our respite caregivers.

"No, I'm your wife."

"Annie," he said, and closed his eyes. After a languid spell, Dick opened his eyes again. He looked at me, and asked, "Who are you?"

I replied impatiently, "Who am I?"

And then he remembered: "Anne-Marie Erickson. My wife."

≈

Commentary: The Scots have a word for it: *tartle*. It can be used as a verb (*to tartle*) or a noun (*a tartle*) to describe that awkward hesitation when we recognize a person, but the name eludes us. Dick would have more such moments. Eventually, it was no longer simply a tartle; sometimes he'd rummage around in his mind for my name and couldn't come up with it.

2011

"I'll never forget you,"
he said on a winter's night
when I tucked him into bed.
Then, as I cuddled up next to him:
"What's your name?"

≈

Commentary: When he'd ask, "Who are you?" I'd tell him that I was his wife, Anne-Marie Erickson. Sometimes, he'd dismiss me, "No, you're not." I was not Anne-Marie Erickson. Alarm would surge through me. "I'm your wife! Anne-Marie Erickson!" I'd yell.

It seemed absurd to be asserting that I was me. It was as if he'd wrested my self from me, a woman who'd spent her adult life trying to move beyond her mother's self-effacement and her father's dismissiveness.

Dick would declare that he was Richard Ralph Cain. He still had a sense of self. But he denied me my identity. Who was I, if not his wife, not Anne-Marie?

≈

When he'd ask, "Who are you?" I learned to move very close to him and look into his eyes.

Then I'd respond to his question with a question: "Who am I?"

"You're my wife, Anne-Marie Erickson!" he'd exclaim, as if I'd just sprung out of the earth.

2011

"I love you," I declared.
"You don't even know me, "
said Dick disdainfully.

≈

Commentary: The English critic Andrew Motion describes the "elusiveness that all human beings detect in one another, no matter how much they love them." Oh how I loved Dick Cain. But how much did we know of one another? After forty-two years together, facets of my husband's inner life still eluded me.

My hands, eyes, mouth, and skin knew his external landscape well. But what can I say about his inner terrain? Could I decipher my beloved's interior, the fault lines and folds, the sediments? Is it possible to read those layers, like a geologist would? Or would I be reading *into* them with my imagination? Wouldn't it be a fabrication, a geologic model fashioned from the malleable putty of guesses and assumptions?

If I'd dug down deep into my husband's subterranean world, could I have unearthed his slumbering six-year-old self, shaped by his mother's screams as they ripped through the night when his father's heart seized and stopped? I visualized that moment when he told me the story, but I never knew the ways in which it may have fashioned fault lines inside him. Did they reveal themselves in the topography of his furrowed brow? In the furrows of his brain?

2012

I told him, "I love you, Dick Cain."
He replied, "I love you, Dick Cain."
I drew in a deep breath, then asked, "Who am I?"
"That's what I'm trying to figure out," he said.

2013

"There are two Annies. You're not the one."
"Who am I then?"
"You'll have to figure that out."

≈

Commentary: My husband and the author James Rufus Agee both were six years old when their fathers died. Agee wrote an evocative autobiographical novel, *A Death in the Family*, about that loss. I read Agee's book when I was an adolescent. His incantatory language captivated me, so I memorized a passage from it. I still can recite it, more than fifty years later. It begins, "Waking in the darkness." A young boy named Rufus has gone to bed on a summer's night in Knoxville. At first, he feels peaceful and secure. Then the darkness moves in closer, enveloping him. Darkness "buried its eye against the eye of the child's own soul." Darkness asked, "Who are you, child, who are you, do you know who you are, do you know who you are, child . . . ?" The darkness of dementia enveloped my husband and me; it buried its cruel eye against our souls and asked that haunting question of us both.

2014
"I don't know who I am."
He'd never said this before.
To my knowledge,
he never said it again.
Fifteen months later
he died.

≈

We are told that St. Francis used to spend whole nights
uttering the same prayer:
"Who are you, O God? And who am I?"

CHAPTER 13

That's Not Becoming of You

"You will not be punished for your anger, you will be punished by your anger." —Gautama Buddha

This essay is about anger. Mine. It's not becoming of me. I must be honest, which means I must be humble. For it's humiliating to tell you about my anger—anger directed at my husband, a man beset by dementia.

I'd told people that writing about anger's fervor and spark would be "fun." When Dick was alive, I'd avow my anger. It was antithetical to resignation, passivity, defeat. Anger has force; I was a woman to be reckoned with.

Then another October blew in, years after his death, his body ash. And memories of my anger toward him became a yoke, biting into my neck.

Some of my anger had been in service of him. It was righteous. I needed to stand up for Dick. But that justifiable temper melded with another: an ire born of impatience, exhaustion, and a hatred of dementia. When angry or weary, I couldn't separate the man from the disease that engulfed him. It felt like a betrayal. He'd become capricious instead of constant.

Now I regret my anger toward him. Many of the words related to *regret* have Latin roots that allude to physical pain: remorse (*remorsus*), "to bite"; compunction (*compungere*), "to sting"; and contrition (*conterere*), "to crush, to grind to pieces." Regret underlies my words, like the notes of a threnody fitted to lyrics. This telling is a form of penance.

≈

In Giotto's frescos of the seven Vices, Anger tears herself apart. All of the Vices are doomed, driven to self-harm. Giotto portrays Anger wrenching open her stola, revealing an emptiness over her heart. The art critic Tom Lubbock observes that Anger's face "smarts from the harm her feelings are doing."

≈

I had reason to be angry. For years, I'd slept lightly, my body attuned to any movement on Dick's side of the bed, my ears alert for the rustling of sheets or a creak in the bed frame. Whenever he got up to go to the bathroom, I, too, arose. Barely awake, I'd grab his hand and lead him there.

Throughout the day, he'd repeat the same question moments after I'd answered it. "Who lives in that yellow house next door?" or "When are we going home?" or "What day is it?" Over and over, I'd reply "The Godfreys," or "At four o'clock," or "Tuesday." It tried my patience.

More than once, I'd searched for his misplaced glasses or his "lost" dentures, which he'd hidden away because they were uncomfortable. I found them in the garbage, the log pile, the plastic bag where I'd stowed my down jacket. "They have to be here somewhere," I'd yell. "What the hell did you do with them?" He'd remain silent, my exasperation seething around him.

≈

At times, my anger flared into a kind of raving madness. I'd scold, snarl, and lash out in a wild fury.

The Furies of mythology emerged from beneath the earth to enforce the proper order of things. They avenged betrayals of primal relationships such as unfilial conduct, patricide, and matricide—crimes of which I was guiltless. But they also avenged "insufficiencies of love." Guilty. And who wouldn't be?

The Furies pursued the culpable. They were curses personified. After Orestes committed matricide, the Furies hounded him. They warned him that he would die "forgotten, without knowing where joy lies anywhere inside your heart."

Their chant was one of "frenzy and fear," their song "binding brain and blighting blood," according to Aeschylus' *Eumenides*. The Furies embodied the bite of remorse, the crush of contrition, the yoke of guilt.

≈

Often, I'd shout because I felt that I was not being heard by Dick or by others. Often, I was fierce. I'd slam doors, pots and pans. I'd pound my fist. I'd curse.

Feeling unheard by medical staff when Dick needed a referral, I swore, hung up the phone, and threw it halfway across the room. Amazingly, it didn't break.

A partial list of objects I broke in anger:

A ceramic cup,

a glass dinner plate,

a wooden salad plate,

a framed photo of Dick and me, and

a full-length mirror that hung inside our bedroom closet door. It came crashing down when I slammed the door shut. It's a piece of evidence, leaning against the garage wall, waiting to be hauled to the dump. It mocks me.

≈

So much pain and anger. Let me pause here for a moment to collect myself. To look out the window at the sun. To leaven my heavy heart.

And yet, I did have reason to be angry.

≈

I'd graded student papers until 4 a.m., then slept briefly. When I got Dick out of bed, the sheets and his pajamas were soaked with urine. I furiously stripped off the bedding, lugged it and his wet pajamas to the washer, cleaned and dressed him, then rushed to work.

When I returned home, I discovered that he'd shit in his shorts.

Exhausted, I lost it. "Damn it! Fuck!"

He said, "We don't use language like that."

"Well, I do when I'm angry. And I'm angry!"

Later that evening, I overheard him in the bedroom reassuring himself: "My dog Phoenix loves me. Annie loves me."

His words stilled the anger churning in my chest; it grew leaden with guilt.

≈

He'd dozed off in front of the television. When he woke up, he asked me, "Who are you?"

"I'm Anne-Marie Erickson, your wife."

He closed his eyes and rested, then opened them again, looked at me, and said, "Ruth Chambers"—the name of his first wife. I repeated my name.

He replied, "Annie is coming here." His eyes alarmed me: flat and dark, their usual gleam gone.

I took his hand in mine. It remained limp. I gave him a hug, a kiss. Still unresponsive. "I'm Annie, your wife," I repeated.

"Annie is coming."

"*I'm* Annie!"

"We'll see."

When I asked him if he'd like to see a photo of the two of us together, he yelled, "No!"

I'd had enough. I abruptly switched off the evening news, then snapped off the lights. "It's time to go to bed."

Just as abruptly, he was back. I was back, too, in his mind. Something in him had switched off, then on. The rest of the evening, he repeated my name and told me that he loved me. The warmth returned to his voice and his eyes.

You forgot my name. That pained me.

Your eyes' lights dimmed. That frightened me.

Forgive me, for I was hurt and afraid.

≈

He'd been awake two nights in a row, hallucinating, gesturing, and talking. I finally moved to the guest room but left the door ajar so I could hear him. I didn't sleep; I listened.

In the middle of the night he swung his arm above his head, knocking loose the framed print of Klimt's "Forest of Beech Trees" that hung above our bed. It swung on one nail.

I removed the print, dressed myself, and dressed him. Then I drove him to the emergency room, worried that an infection might have caused delirium.

The young male nurse advised me that, since Dick had dementia, I should not leave objects where he might "tamper" with them. As if I'd not lived with my husband's dementia for many years already. As if the shelves and walls in our beautiful home ought to be stark, barren of any art.

My vocal chords tightened, closing off a wail: "Please don't advise me! Please don't pretend to understand! You do not—can not—understand!"

But I was too weary to tell him this.

≈

Dick would spit onto the carpet, his chair, and the tawny walls at the assisted living home where he resided during the last two years of his life. The aides or I would wipe up the thick spittle.

I'd hold a tissue in front of his mouth when he'd clear his throat. "Please spit here, into this," I'd direct him. More than once, he'd grabbed my wrist and yanked my hand away, then spat onto the floor. It infuriated me. I needed to step out of his room to calm down. I had to remove myself from his presence.

After Dick died, I noticed traceries of spit on the wall behind his bed. I scrubbed them away with vehemence.

Tell me, did I have reason to be angry?

He'd shit on the toilet seat, the floor, my hand. He was oblivious. I cursed.

He asked me, "Why do you use those words?"

"Because I'm angry. That's the language I use when I'm angry."

"Well, that's not becoming of you."

≈

While I was helping Dick with his toileting, he ordered me: "You can leave now."

"I'm your fucking wife. I'm not leaving."

"No, you aren't my wife. You swear too much."

"I swear because I'm upset. You're home, with me, your wife."

"You're lost. You don't know where you are."

"You're the one who's lost!" I yelled. "Look at me! I'm your wife! Annie."

"Hi, Annie!"

Later, I'd apologize for losing my temper. "You did?" He didn't remember.

We're counseled to forgive and forget. He'd already forgotten, so there was nothing to forgive.

I have not forgotten. Forgive me.

≈

For years, Dick had a litany of swear words he'd use in anger: "God-damn-fucking-son-of-a-bitch." It had a jagged rhythm, the chugging of a locomotive as it picked up speed.

Cursing is not the sole preserve of men, as if a boundary existed between the male realm of expletives and some lady-land, the domain of decorous language. Dick had agreed with me. He'd always been polite, but he didn't put much stock in proprieties.

So who was this man chiding me, "That's not becoming of you" and informing me that "we don't use language like that"? Who was this royal "we"? Who was this stranger?

IN THE EVENING, WE'LL DANCE

≈

The anthropologist Colin Turnbull reported that the Mbuti people of the Congo envisioned a sphere that surrounded each person, moving with and protecting him or her. However, people would become *wazi-wazi*—"disoriented, and unpredictable"—if they arrived at the sphere's boundary before the center had time to catch up. If the movement from their sphere's center was too violent, a person might "pierce through into the other world." At times, Dick seemed to be in another world. It was as if he'd lost his center; he became unpredictable.

When Dick momentarily became *wazi-wazi*, you could say that he was possessed. But there's no exorcism that can cast out the demon dementia.

≈

Two years before Dick died, I dreamed that he was in bed with me, facing my back, nestled. I felt his warmth, his body pressing against mine—a feeling I'd loved. He wrapped both of his arms around me.

Then, he held my wrists. I couldn't free my hands. I pleaded with him, "Please, let go. Let go of at least one of my hands."

I panicked. He was holding me too closely, too tightly. "Let go! Let go!"

Finally, I woke. I wondered if the staff at the care facility would call to inform me that Dick had died. I doubted it; I'd asked him to let go of only one hand, not both.

I left a lamp on the rest of the night. I didn't want the dream to return. Even though I thought it was Dick next to me, the fear was of a stranger.

Forgive me, for I was afraid of this stranger.

≈

Days of chaos supplanted our pleasant, ordered life. The man I'd known for decades grew erratic. I seldom could reason with him. He was, at times, irascible, resistant, or intemperate—and no longer able to ask for forgiveness. He used to be the first to do so.

It's not intentional. It's the disease.

It's not intentional. It's the disease.

It takes a long time to truly inhabit this idea. It takes a long time to realize that dementia burns all the bridges; there's no going back to who he was. I was the one who had to change. He couldn't. It's the disease.

Forgive me, for I did not know.

≈

In the past, during an argument, Dick would leave our cabin, stride up the long path through the hayfield and onto the county road. He'd walk until he'd cooled off. When he'd recovered his calm, he'd return home and apologize.

As the dementia progressed, there were times when I wished that he'd walk out like he used to—walk out into the bitter night, into the snow-filled forest. Get lost. And never return.

I was—we were—at the edge of a madness. I'd imagine taking his hand and walking together to the yard's verge, then into those winter woods. I'd imagine taking his hand and walking together from the shore's edge into the shallows and then the depths of Lake Superior. To end it, for him and for me.

Forgive me, for I, too, was lost.

≈

We'd entered uncharted territory. Living with dementia is an irrational experience, as the writer Pauline Boss points out. Dementia is strange and unsettling. Boss says it's "uncanny." The uncanny makes us uneasy. Dick made some people uneasy. They told me that being with him was "difficult," so they'd disengage from him.

I wanted to shout at them, but instead I explained. Cited research. Recounted his amusing or amazing remarks.

I admit that I lacked empathy during those encounters. In my anger, I wanted to shake them, rattling their bones. I imagined that I'd reveal a hole where their heart was supposed to be.

Forgive me, for I felt heartsick and so alone.

≈

"Fear seeks noisy company and pandemonium to scare away the demons." —Carl Jung

The uncanny engenders fear. And anger is often the "offspring of fear . . . fear at one's own human vulnerability," observes the philosopher Martha Nussbaum. I felt defenseless against dementia—its capriciousness, its ruthless force, its inexorability. When we're beset by fears, anger "gives the illusion of agency and control." I grabbed onto it, like an iron bar on a whirling merry-go-round.

When threatened, our basic reaction is to either freeze, flee, or fight. Because I was Dick's caregiver, I couldn't freeze. And I couldn't flee, either, although some counseled "divorce him" when the money started to run out. I ignored them.

Hence, it came down to anger, the fuel for the fight. Anger triggers instinctive reactions, such as alertness and a swift response. By its very nature, "anger is hostile to understanding. . . . It's not for nothing that we call rages 'blind,'" observes Rebecca Solnit in her essay, "Facing the Furies."

I know a bit about blind rage. When we were children, a friend teased my sister. I stepped in to defend her, stepped within inches of our friend, so enraged that I didn't even see her face. I saw only a scrim of white.

My rages toward Dick also were blind. They had to have been. If I'd truly seen him in his lostness and vulnerability, I couldn't have cursed at him. If I'd truly seen his love and need for me, I couldn't have raged on.

In the midst of my outbursts, sometimes I would look into his eyes. Then I would embrace him and weep, inconsolable.

≈

A year after Dick's death, I read Nussbaum's essay. She writes that anger can be "an alluring substitute for grieving." I'd witnessed my beloved's losses due to dementia—one loss and then another, year after year. For seventeen years before my widowhood, I was beset with grief.

I'm still learning how to forgive myself.

CHAPTER 14

Annie, Can We Be Done with This Now?

In myths and fairy tales, the hero must tackle daunting trials, such as slaying a monster, spinning straw into gold, or knitting shirts out of stinging nettles. A guide or helper often appears to aid her or him. The guide may arrive in the form of ants, a fish, frog, river reed, crone, drum, or fairy godmother.

Like a fairy tale's beleaguered hero, I faced taxing trials while living with Dick's dementia. Sometimes my husband came to my rescue.

≈

Dick slept a lot during the final years of his life. When he was still at home, sometimes I'd spend an hour or more trying to get him up. One spring day, I called to him and kissed his eyelids. Then I exclaimed, "Sunshine!" as I opened the curtains.

Usually when I said the word *sunshine*, he'd begin singing, "You Are My Sunshine." Not that morning. "Close them! It hurts my eyes," he yelled. I complied.

I waited a while, then yanked his bedcovers off. "Please get up! I have to go to work," I pleaded. I needed to assist him with dressing, toileting, and taking his medications before the respite aide arrived.

Finally, he let me help him out of bed, guide him to the bathroom, and ready him for the day. Finally, I settled him into a chair by the kitchen table while I prepared his breakfast.

Still fuming, I slammed cupboard doors. I banged a pot onto the stovetop. I stirred his hot cereal with a metal spoon; the din grated on my ears. On his, too, I hoped. He loathed loud noises.

He sat at the table, placidly waiting for breakfast. I thought he'd tuned out the noise. Then he said, "Annie, can we be done with this now?"

I stopped stirring and went to him. I wrapped my arms around him, kissed him, and said, "Yes, love, we can be done with this." This racket. This anger.

He'd come to my rescue again. With that simple question, he allayed my anger.

More than once, he disarmed me of my ire by declaring, "But I love you." When Dick reminded me of the person I loved, he also summoned up the person he loved.

I wept with remorse when I described this scene to my therapist. She reassured me that I had reason to be angry, then added, "Not everyone is married to the Dalai Lama."

≈

Once a dream served as my guide:

I dreamed that I stood in a subterranean space: an empty concrete basement with stark grey walls and floor. Plastic covered the single small window. Dim light diffused through it.

A creature appeared at the window. It was a large wolverine, dark brown with buff-colored stripes running along its sides. He was scratching at the plastic sheeting with his sharp claws, trying to get in. It frightened me.

Suddenly, he stopped his clawing. He reached down and picked up a large dusky-gold egg. An evergreen bush stood to his left. The wolverine set the egg in the shrub's lower branches.

My eyes followed that egg and forgot the fear.

IN THE EVENING, WE'LL DANCE

≈

When I awoke, I was certain the dream-creature was a wolverine, although I'd never actually seen one. Nor was I aware of the Wolverine of Marvel Comics and X-Men movies.

Curious, I viewed online photos of wolverines. The animal's size, dark-brown color, and the stripes along its sides assured me that the creature in my dream was a wolverine.

Wolverines are furtive and fierce. Because they seem both mysterious and menacing, they're the subject of legends and fears. In 1979, an article in a Colorado newspaper described them as "something out of a nightmarish fairy tale."

Contemporary researchers who study the creature have arrived at a more nuanced portrayal. Maurice Hornocker, who conducted a long-term study of wolverines, said, "We gained tremendous respect for the animal's tenacity, determination, strength and endurance."

≈

The wolverine dream came during the difficult middle phase of Dick's dementia. I was desperate for a way out of my vexation and ill humor. For days afterward, I puzzled over the curious images—the wolverine, the bush, the egg. What truths or insights were they leading me toward?

I'd found myself facing a feral animal. The psychologist James Hillman says that animal dreams "really wake people up . . . [and] get them thinking, interested, and curious." He suggests that we ought to ask, "Why did it bother to come to me?"

At first, I thought the wolverine was merely a manifestation of my wrath. Like a cornered animal, I'd often lash out. My anger was born of fear, but also of resistance: to the tasks of caring for Dick, to the restriction of my freedoms, and to the disease itself.

The insistent, clawing creature would not be denied. I found myself cornered. I decided to let in the dream-creature so it could guide me. At first, I saw only the wolverine's fierceness—and mine.

≈

The wolverine places an egg in the evergreen bush. Evergreens are symbolic of protection. Birds will build nests and shelter in their dense foliage. In my dream, the bush's branches protect the nestled egg.

And what of that golden egg? It seemed bizarre, even laughable, when I first wrote about it in my journal. Then I read that an egg symbolizes potentiality. The golden egg shone against the dark pelage of the creature and the shrub's deep green leaves. It lit up that underground space.

The wolverine had left me with a golden egg, as if to tell me, "The strength you need is within you."

≈

The creature ceased his clawing and shifted his attention to the egg, which he tended to with care. The dream caused a shift in me, too. I gradually learned to rein in my wrath and turn my attention to my husband, to my love.

My dream was a turning point. It reminded me that I needn't be enslaved by my anger and plight. I, too, possessed the wolverine's courage and strengths. Those traits helped me through the trials that were to come. My spirit would remain unbroken.

≈

The wolverine dream was like a slap that woke me up. It caused me to revise how I viewed Dick's dementia, my anger, and myself. This is not to say that the change in me was sudden or complete. My equanimity would wobble, like the bubble in a spirit level I'd used to scribe the logs for our cabin. At times, I'd shift out of true. But as the years wore on, more often than not, I stayed centered and held steady in my fierce love for Dick.

CHAPTER 15

I Can't Avoid Moving on to the Horror

In 2017, a fisherman drowned on the Mississippi River, sucked underwater at Lock and Dam No. 8 near Genoa, Wisconsin. Moments before the boat went down, the man rushed to put on his life jacket. He lowered the anchor. It didn't hold. The dam's churn "was too strong," said the sheriff. It pulled the boat under.

I wanted to understand how that could have happened, so I watched an online video, "The Danger of Dams," created by a Pennsylvania TV news team. They'd positioned a boat downriver from a roller dam, with a camera strapped to the stern and a mannequin at the prow. The aluminum boat floated toward the dam, then crashed over the dam's roller. Roiling water slammed into it, and the mannequin flailed about. Seething waves battered the small vessel, quickly filling it. It keeled over, sucked under in a thunder of water. The underwater footage lasts two minutes but seems much longer: the water's constant roar, flurries of ripples and bubbles, glimpses of yellow light, spells of blackness.

I forced myself to watch it all. It seemed illustrative of how Dick might have felt. He flailed about, but dementia's currents were too strong. It sucked him under, into the tumult. During those spells of blackness, I could read the panic in his eyes.

Sometimes I was able to anchor him. Sometimes, the anchor didn't hold.

ANNE-MARIE ERICKSON

≈

On a night in late November of 2005, I drove through the aftermath of a blizzard, the furrow of road bounded by looming hummocks of snow. At times I drove blind, visibility lost in whiteouts when winds churned up the snow.

All day, I'd stayed with Dick in his room at the local hospital. I sat by the window and watched rain turn to snow. At six that evening, he was discharged. The staff wouldn't let Dick stay another night, despite his anxiety, despite the fact that my six-foot-tall husband weighed only 135 pounds.

He refused to eat, fearful food would get stuck in his throat. There was no organic cause. He had phagophobia, "fear of swallowing," an anxiety that causes the throat muscles to contract. Dick's fear foreshadowed the final stages of dementia. It was as if he'd had a premonition; a decade later, he was physically unable to swallow. He'd choke on a sip of water.

The only option, the doctor said, was for me to take him to a geriatric psychiatric unit an hour away. We went home, packed a few of his things, and left for Bemidji. The car cleaved the snow, plowing into the dark night that lay beyond the headlights. I couldn't see the road ahead.

≈

Dick was admitted for anxiety and depression. The staff noted that he had "grief related to his memory disturbance." He expressed "feelings of hopelessness and worthlessness." He felt defeated.

Dick remained hospitalized in a locked ward for fourteen days. The walls of his narrow room were pale green—a green with the life drained out of it. A streetlight outside the single window gave off a sallow glow.

During that time, he wrote many notes to me. They read like desperate dispatches from a drowning man, as my husband struggled against dementia's strong pull. On December 1, he wrote, "I don't know what happened, but I wound up at the place shown on the return address, 'Senior Behavioral Healthcare Unit.' I love you so much and all our kids and relatives. I'm so lonely. Love, Dick."

A note written on December 2 begins in a firm cursive, "Annie, my love, my love, my love." As the message tumbles down the page, his script grows tight. The ragged letters seem to tremble: "I can't avoid moving on to the horror. I'm afraid."

In the upper margins of an entry dated December 10, he printed the words *hurt* and *pain*. Underneath that, he wrote an abridged version of a passage from Hamlet's soliloquy. Dick had committed it to memory almost six decades earlier, in a high school English class. *Whether tis nobler in the mind to suffer the slings & arrows of outrageous fortune or by opposing end them.*

A few pages later, he reiterated the passage in a smaller script. He followed it with *I want to die.* On the next page, he wrote: *And and and as I leave, I worry what this will do to my loved ones.*

≈

The author Olivia Ames Hoblitzelle describes a similar despair in the life of her husband, Harrison, who had Alzheimer's. A few years after his diagnosis, he spoke up at a small gathering of family and friends. He considered the possibility that it was "time for me to get off the bus." He explained, "It's getting really hard, and I guess the time comes when it's just not worth it anymore." Harrison's circle of loving confidants convinced him that it wasn't yet time.

It got really hard for Dick, too, during the middle phase of his dementia. A month prior to his stay at the Bemidji facility, he'd been hospitalized for dehydration. He told me that I must be strong. I asked him why. "Because I'm dying," he said. "It's cruel, so cruel."

The doctor had prescribed Seroquel, explaining that it usually helped the elderly with anxiety. It delivered Dick to a hellish pit. I read poems aloud, hoping that the music of poetry might soothe him. His ears were sealed to words he'd always savored. His eyes grew dark; no light shone from them.

In the following weeks, Dick hid the kitchen knives, fearing he'd harm himself. He didn't want to sleep in our loft, fearing that he'd jump out of it. In December, he took a run at a window in the psych unit.

He also banged his head against a wall, in hopes of ending it all.

≈

How calmly 2005 seemed to have begun, based on the entries in my engagement calendar. I was trying to live as we'd always done, trying to hold it together as it fell apart. *Trying*: The word I often uttered over the seventeen years of his decline.

My calendar contains observations about eagles, owls, redpolls, snowfalls, and ice storms. Notes about cooking stews and soups. Plans for movie, concert, and dinner dates with friends. Most entries are plural: *we cook, we ski at dusk, we cull through books*. But many of them switch to the first person singular: *I buy snow tires for the car. I shovel. I haul in the water.*

Beneath a seemingly stable surface, our lives had begun to spin out, as if we were steel balls caught inside a pinball machine. An invisible hand triggered levers that swatted at us and set us spinning.

Recently, I happened upon photos taken of me taken during that period: a smile beneath fear-filled eyes. The discordance startled me.

≈

I've heard people say that living with dementia is harder on the loved ones than on the person who has it. How can they possibly know this? Perhaps it's easier for them to imagine the loved one's plight than that of the person with dementia. Perhaps people want—need, even—to identify with the healthy spouse because the prospect of dementia terrifies them.

Given what I witnessed, I believe that living with dementia often is harder on the person who has it. As Steve Gentleman, a neuropathologist, points out, "To be in a body whose brain is failing and still have insight into what is going on must be simply horrendous."

I couldn't know Dick's inmost thoughts, but his own writings reveal what it was like for him during his decline. I found them when I leafed through his old planners, searching for clues. Over the years, Dick had kept daily calendars. In 2005, he completed the last of them. By 2006, he was unable to continue.

It's painful for me to page through his planner for 2005. His entries began with a list of books he wanted to read, including *Instead of Violence, Homage to Catalonia,* and *Irish Women: Image and Achievement,* as well as two studies of intellectual history. The volumes piled on his desk gradually became studded with torn scraps of paper.

To this day, I'll pull one of his books off a shelf and find it littered with bits of paper, marking pages. On some of those pages, he'd underlined almost every sentence. He couldn't remember what he'd just read. He couldn't follow the line of thought.

≈

Throughout 2005, Dick's planner reveals an escalating disorder. In January, his writing escapes the lined pages, spills into the borders, and sometimes runs sideways. Pages are strewn with script and underlining. He drew red or green arrows to guide himself through his notes. He got the date of a trip to Duluth wrong, drew red arrows that directed him to the next page, added "mañana."

He'd list friends to whom he wanted to write. Again and again. He repeated "Write letter to Isaac" six times. The letters weren't being written. At one point, he decided to write to our dog: "Write letter to Phoenix." He entered it three times.

The notes in his planner—about a photo shoot, a meeting to be covered for the local newspaper, garden and household chores—grew more chaotic as the year progressed. By September, what had been his book also became mine. I jotted down reminders: his appointments, my teaching schedule at the college, phone calls he needed to make.

A small drawing—sketched on April 29, three days after his seventy-third birthday—is emblematic of the entire book, of the entire year. In one corner of a cluttered page, he'd depicted a man's face. The man's mouth is agape, brows lowered, eyes wide, with two question marks above the head and one on the forehead.

≈

Each day, each moment, presents us with a flood of incoming information—a flood that Dick's brain could no longer control. His entries in October and November reflect his distress. Like the drowning fisherman, he struggled to put on a life jacket. He told me, "I'm battling to keep my spirits up."

He directed himself, "My anxiety. Turn mind away from this." He created lists:

- *Eat*
- *Exercise*
- *Do stretches*
- *Study Spanish*
- *Drawings—Do some!*
- *Help Annie out*
- *Use brain*

He counseled himself: "Thinking Problems? Eat more and read. When have negative thoughts, eat more and read *Enlightened Heart* and *Earth Prayers*."

He was trying to hang on.

≈

Surgery was the tipping point. Dick's health declined markedly after surgery for an enlarged prostate in September of 2005. It pushed him beyond coping, deeper into the dementia.

In the months following the surgery, Dick often "wasn't up to it"—harvesting the root vegetables, going with me to a bookstore, attending my nephew's wedding. He felt "rotten." He was pale, weak, achy, and lightheaded. He suffered from frequent prostate and urinary tract infections, which triggered dehydration. Dehydration can lead to disorientation, particularly if a person has dementia.

I think of this as the period of the "*d*-words," including *d*ementia, of course, as well as *d*ehydration, *d*epression, *d*elusions, *d*ecline, *d*istress, and thought *d*isorders, such as *d*elirium, hallucinations, and psychotic episodes. Agitation and violence sometimes followed.

The word *delirium* comes from the Latin *delirare*, meaning to be "crazy or to rave." It's a sudden state of severe confusion. When my mother was in her early nineties, she had a fainting spell due to dehydration. She was hospitalized overnight. My sister got a call at midnight. Mother was roaming the hallways, hitting people, yelling, and swearing—a woman whose usual expletive was "Uff da!" My sister said that Mother "was not in reality." She was in delirium.

During hospitalizations, it's quite common for the elderly to enter into delirium. It can be caused by the disorientation of being in an unfamiliar place, by too much noise overloading the brain, or by pain. Unlike Dick, Mother didn't have dementia. If a person already has dementia, delirium can accelerate the decline in memory and thinking skills.

≈

One of the first episodes of a thought disorder occurred after Dick's prostate surgery. He broke down crying. He told me, "I've lost all control. I'm afraid." He feared he was losing his mind. He'd hear voices. They'd get stuck in a loop. It's known as perseveration, the repetition of words. The person is unable to switch ideas.

The narcotic hydrocodone, prescribed for his post-operative pain, is a disinhibitor, so Dick's already-frail brain couldn't suppress those obsessive thoughts. One of the voices told him:

Throwyourmittensonthefloor!Throwyourmittensonthefloor!Throwyourmittensonthefloor!
Throwyourmittensonthefloor!Throwyourmittensonthefloor!Throwyourmittensonthefloor!
Throwyourmittensonthefloor!Throwyourmittensonthefloor!Throwyourmittensonthefloor!

Although I was amused by the content of the message, I didn't let on. He was in too much distress. I tried to calm him. I played soothing music, rubbed his back, and talked with him, attempting to replace those inner voices with dialogue.

≈

That October, Dick harbored the belief that our drinking water was poisonous. He soon recognized that as "a crazy idea." He was deluded. In fact, delusions are quite common in persons with dementia. They usually manifest in the middle to late stages, when a person is struggling to make sense of his or her world while dealing with memory loss, cognitive decline, and the concomitant confusion and fear.

Most of Dick's delusions were harmless. A few of them seemed like a form of wish fulfillment. Several times, he announced, "I'm President of the United States of America." Dick always had been politically involved, but he'd never run for office. He also declared that he'd written *For Whom the Bell Tolls*. Although he took pride in being a journalist, early in our relationship, Dick told me that he wished he'd written some fiction.

≈

In addition to delusions, Dick experienced hallucinations. Both conditions involve the loss of contact with reality. The difference is that delusions involve false beliefs that aren't consistent with reality, while hallucinations are based on sensory perceptions, according to the Alzheimer's Association. Dick would hear or see things that weren't there.

For several years after his prostate surgery, the hallucinations were auditory. He'd hear voices, especially when he was anxious. The voices told him to "shut up" or called him "an asshole." They also informed him that someone wanted to kill him. He asked me, "Do we have a gun?" He believed that his antagonist was lurking in our house. He needed to defend himself.

Near the end of Dick's life, the voices ceased. Instead, he experienced visual illusions. They were benign. He'd often look at the ceiling while hallucinating. I'd ask him what he saw up there. Once, he told me he saw Hungries. Another time, it was a Pinkerinie. (How I wish I could have seen the Pinkerinie!) He also told me, "I see fields." I asked him if they were pretty. He replied, "Extraordinarily."

One morning he told me that he'd seen angels. Later on, he stared open-mouthed at the ceiling while resting in his bed. He was transfixed by whatever it was he saw above him. The thing I couldn't see. Another enchanting field? Another angel, hovering above him, watching over his still body?

Dick's hallucinations were caused by an organic psychosis. Organic psychoses can be associated with drug use, delirium, or medical conditions such as dementia, according to the neurologist Oliver Sacks. Fortunately, they are transient.

≈

When I hear the words *delusion* and *hallucination*, I think of psychosis. In fact, psychosis occurs in up to fifty percent of dementia cases, according to a 2019 report in the medical journal *Translational Psychiatry*. Psychotic episodes in persons with dementia include sporadic hallucinations (auditory or visual) and delusions.

If Dick was disturbed by a delusion, I'd try to redirect him. I would talk about our dog Phoenix, sing Dick's favorite songs, or suggest we go for a walk. If his delusions were benign, I'd ask questions. I was curious. I wanted to learn more, to participate with him in his imaginings. Our excursions were brief; I knew that he'd soon reenter reality.

Witnessing my husband's psychotic states didn't particularly alarm me. Psychosis had been normalized for me as a child. My great-aunt Martha was institutionalized for much of her adult life. She had catatonic schizophrenia. On rare occasions, the family would "get Martha out" so she could join us for a reunion.

I don't recall Martha speaking or even moving from her chair, although she must have dined with us. Stout and mute, she seemed in a torpor. I was fascinated by her, rather than frightened, perhaps because the adults seemed comfortable with her presence.

≈

It wasn't delirium, delusions, or hallucinations that brought Dick and me to the emergency room on September 19, 2006. It was agitation and violence. Late at night, I drove Dick to the hospital from our home in the countryside. We walked hand in hand through the chilly ambulance garage. I pressed the buzzer to be admitted. A nurse let us in.

We sat side by side on the examination table, silent, still holding hands. A police officer arrived, spoke quietly to the doctor, then hovered at a distance from us, watching. Eventually, the officer determined that he wasn't needed. He left.

Throughout that day, Dick had been agitated. He searched for the car keys. It perturbed him that his driving privileges had been revoked. He had skillfully navigated the freeways when we lived in or visited the Twin Cities. During the earlier stages of dementia, he'd driven the seven miles from our cabin into Deer River for daily visits with his aunt Doris. But in August of 2006 his geriatric psychiatrist informed us that Dick had "probable Alzheimer's" and could no longer drive. He denied the diagnosis—yelling "Not Alzheimer's!" when I told a friend. He also wouldn't accept that he couldn't drive.

That evening, Dick grew increasingly distraught as he searched for the spare set of car keys. I'd hidden them. While I busied myself with grading student papers, he rummaged in his cluttered desk, looking for the keys.

Suddenly, I realized that he wasn't in the house. I ran outside. He was seated in the car, in the driver's seat. Had he found the keys I'd hidden? Had he taken mine from my purse? I had no idea.

I stood beside the car, pleading with Dick to get out. He refused. I coaxed. He refused. I yelled. He refused. There was no one within earshot. Our cabin was in the middle of twenty acres of land on a dead-end county road. Woods loomed to the south and east; sere fields spread out to the west and north. Our isolation unsettled me.

Finally, I opened the door and yanked Dick out of the car. He stumbled and fell against a rick of logs. I helped him up. As we walked to the cabin, Dick pushed me, mirroring my angry gesture with his own. I fell backwards, hitting my head on the wooden fence.

In our many years together, he'd never harmed me in any way. That act stunned me more than the blow to my head. It must have stunned him, too, because he calmed down.

Together, we went into the house and pulled on our jackets. Then we got into the car and headed to the emergency room. I drove.

IN THE EVENING, WE'LL DANCE

≈

I can't justify my behavior that night, but I want to understand it. I'd read the advice for caregivers: When a person with dementia is agitated, *don't* shout, *don't* show fear or alarm, *don't* initiate physical contact. I failed; I *did* all of the *don'ts*. I remember my reaction when I first read those tips: "Sure. And then you can apply for sainthood."

Once again, I'd lost it. If we "lose it," the *it* we lose is our self-control. I lost it that night because panic got the better of me. *Panic* derives from the half-man, half-goat Greek god of the wild, Pan. Pan clouds the borderline between the rational human and the inner beast that we bridle within our psyches.

Like anger, panic is so powerful that it overwhelms reason. That night, a wild panic crouched inside me, ready to spring.

≈

I agreed with the ER physician that Dick needed to be hospitalized again. This time, they sedated my husband and an ambulance delivered him to the facility in Bemidji. I visited him the next evening after work. He was affectionate but muzzy from the psychotropic drugs prescribed for him.

When I left, the heavy door locked behind me. Dick pressed his face against a window in the door, panic in his eyes. I forced myself to turn my back on him.

All hell broke loose after that, according to a nurse I spoke with the next morning. Dick was up all night. He'd barricaded himself in the shower room. He'd torn things off walls. I never asked her what he'd damaged. I didn't want to know. If the images were too vivid, they'd bedevil me.

He didn't sleep for thirty-two hours. The staff tried various drugs to calm him. He remained guarded. He paced the floor and peered around corners. After eight days, he showed little improvement. They told me that he wasn't stable and needed "secure placement." I decided to move him to the geriatric psychiatric unit at Mayo Clinic in Rochester.

ANNE-MARIE ERICKSON

≈

When he was admitted to Mayo on September 21, the summary diagnosis included depression, delirium, behavioral dyscontrol, and aggression. He was combative, kicking and striking out. His behavior was "guarded and threatening." He "appeared to respond to unseen stimuli." At times, he required physical restraints, observation, or seclusion.

They'd put him in seclusion because he'd hit a nurse. They feared for the safety of the elderly patients in the ward. His doctors tried a number of psychotropic drugs with no success. They'd run out of options. They needed my consent to start electroconvulsive therapy (ECT).

I hesitated.

≈

The name itself made me hesitate. Electroconvulsive therapy is commonly referred to as "electroshock" or "shock treatment." *Shock* is from an Old German word, *scoc*, which means *jolt*. It conjures up the image of a lightning bolt.

The writer Sylvia Plath was given ECT as a young woman. She wrote about it in *The Bell Jar,* a novel, as well as in a poem, "The Hanging Man": "By the roots of my hair some god got hold of me. / I sizzled in his blue volts."

I hesitated because of the outdated images I retained. All I knew of ECT were the depictions I'd read in Plath's works and seen in movies such as *The Snake Pit* and *One Flew Over the Cuckoo's Nest.*

In films, ECT is portrayed as barbaric and terrifying. A screaming patient pleads, "No, don't do this to me!" Then he or she is strapped to a table, leather restraints on arms and legs, a stick or rag shoved between the teeth. A nurse utters soothing words while a doctor turns knobs on a black machine, the dials displaying increasingly strong jolts of electricity.

The patient, conscious and wide-eyed, convulses wildly, as if having a grand mal seizure. Ominous music plays in the background. In one film, the screen is suffused with a red glow during the treatment.

IN THE EVENING, WE'LL DANCE

≈

When I took the call from Mayo's psychiatric ward, I was in my college office—270 miles away. I'd just returned from Rochester the previous night. The doctor wanted to start ECT right away, but agreed to wait. Late that night, I returned to Rochester.

The next morning, a psychiatric nurse explained to me that ECT is advised when no other treatment has been effective. It's used as a last resort. Unlike the obsolete images I'd seen in movies, the ECT administered today is considered safe and effective. The patient is not conscious. He or she receives a short-acting anesthesia, as well as a muscle relaxant that reduces the severity of convulsions. The pulses of electricity and the seizures they cause are brief.

ECT is used for people suffering from depression, catatonia, or mania—and for dementia patients in distress who have treatment-resistant depression, agitation, or aggression. When a dementia patient has ECT, it causes the depression to lift and "confusion and cognitive impairment also improve," reports George Grossberg, a geriatric psychiatrist. Psychiatrists don't know why ECT works, only that it seems to cause changes in brain chemistry that can quickly reverse symptoms.

≈

I gave my permission. The following morning, Dick was wheeled into a small room next to the ECT suite. I held his hand while an IV was inserted. This was not the usual protocol, but his doctors knew my presence would be helpful. Dick would be less resistant.

A few years later, when he received ECT as an outpatient, I couldn't accompany him. A nurse wheeled Dick directly into the ECT room. I followed with my eyes. As the door closed, I saw his feet, shod in white tennis shoes, frantically flailing. I've not been able to erase that picture from my memory. It torments me still.

I never witnessed what followed: the electrode pads being placed on his temples; the mouth guard inserted to protect his teeth and tongue; the brief seizure that caused his muscles to convulse as electrical currents passed through his brain.

Dick had twenty-one ECT treatments at Mayo Clinic: sixteen between 2006 and 2008 and five more in 2013. Usually, he'd improve after three, administered every other day. In 2008, his psychiatrist recommended maintenance ECT. Every month for five years, I drove Dick to a hospital in Duluth for his outpatient treatments.

ECT has been described as an "electrical storm" which causes brain cells to fire at high rates. After the ECT he was much calmer. For a few days, he also was more mentally alert. Like a lightning strike, it briefly lit up the abraded terrain of his frail brain.

Then, about a week prior to his next appointment, he'd grow agitated once again.

≈

The word *violence* seemed less frightening when I learned that it originates from the Latin *violentia,* "vehemence." Vehemence is a display of strong feeling. I think that best describes the agitated behavior of persons who have dementia. They can't explain what is disturbing them, but they urgently want it to stop.

Often, a person with dementia is reacting to a trigger. It might be fear, frustration, boredom, confusion, pain, illness, or even a urinary tract infection. The aggression might be physical—kicking, hitting, throwing or breaking things—or verbal, such as shouting and swearing. However, medical specialists note that it's rare that people who have dementia will resort to extreme violence and seriously harm someone.

There's some evidence that anxiety and depression tend to be more common in the early to middle stages of dementia, while behavioral problems such as aggression occur in the more advanced phases. As his dementia progressed, at times Dick's rages were due to illness, confusion, or fear. Sometimes, he simply needed to assert himself—to determinedly, obstinately remain himself.

However, as a person becomes increasingly impaired, "some behavioral dysfunctions get gradually less problematic," according to Franz Müller-Spahn, a Swiss psychiatrist. A kind of peace may prevail. Thankfully, this is what I witnessed in my husband.

≈

Others told me about the aggression of their loved ones who had dementia. They looked me in the eyes and spoke in quiet, restrained voices. Given what they told me, their calm seemed incongruous—as if they were recounting someone else's story.

A neighbor told me that she had to call the police several times because her husband had violently resisted her when she tried to assist him in the bathroom. She also had to lock him in their bedroom at night. She slept in the safety of the guest room.

Our friend Joyce described the night she stayed with her mother at a care facility. Her mother desperately wanted to go home. She repeatedly walked into a wall, attempting to pass through it to get home. Concerned that her mother would injure herself, Joyce managed to get her seated. She placed a pillow on her mother's lap. Then she laid her own head and upper body firmly on top of the pillow to restrain her. Joyce repeatedly explained to her mother that she needed to do this so she wouldn't injure herself. The mother yanked at her daughter's long hair, scratched her arms, hit her. All night long, our friend held on despite her mother's fury.

≈

We hold within us a multiplicity of selves, some dormant, some active, some that show up in our dreams or sneak up on us. Child-selves still reside within us—the one fearing abandonment, the one enthralled by the sensory world, the one angry at being misunderstood or ignored. We harbor our youthful selves, struggling or rebellious, dreamy or adrift. We also may conceal aspects of our self due to societal or familial pressures. As dementia progresses through the years—or even moves through a person's days—those selves might suddenly appear.

Individuals with dementia usually lose their most recent memories first, then gradually move back in time. They may think a loved one, such as a daughter, is their deceased mother. In the middle phase of his dementia, Dick relived memories from his twenties, of a long-ago love affair. Near the end of his life, he asked me if I would take him to

Minneapolis to visit his parents. I responded with an evasion, telling him that it was too late in the day for such a long trip. Dick's parents had been dead for more than fifty years, but in his mind he'd become their child once again.

Gisela Webb, a scholar of religions, wrote about her own mother, who had Alzheimer's. During the six years her mother lived in a nursing home, Webb also came to know the other residents. She says that she "felt as if I were gaining glimpses of their inner lives and perhaps past experiences." They appeared to be reliving or processing facets of their pasts, including the old angers, wounds, and griefs.

An acquaintance told me about his mother's fury after she'd developed dementia. I wondered if her rage might have surfaced as she relived past wounds.

The man said that such anger was not characteristic of the woman he knew. He noted that she'd had a difficult childhood and early adulthood. Later in life, she became fiercely determined to better her lot. She fought to become a respected professional, earning an advanced degree while in her forties.

When she had dementia, she was often belligerent and foulmouthed, according to her distraught son. Perhaps those were the rants of a wounded child. Or perhaps her warrior-self reappeared to do battle against dementia.

≈

I wanted to tell you that the violence ended with the ECT. And it did—towards me. But Dick occasionally would yell at or hit staff in the hospital or assisted living home.

I wanted to tell you that after 2005-2007, our life together calmed down. I believed that it had. Then I read his discharge summaries from Mayo's geriatric psychiatric unit:

June 2008 - Worsening psychotic symptoms, paranoia, rumination, hallucinations.

July 2011 - Transient auditory hallucinations, confusion, disorientation, word-finding difficulties.

January 2013 - Mutism, confusion, visual hallucinations.

April 2013 - Worsening visual hallucinations and psychosis, behavioral dyscontrol.

When I began writing this essay, I found that I'd forgotten events and confused the ones I did remember. When was Dick's surgery? The first trip to Mayo Clinic? When was it that he had the swallowing anxiety? In what year was our fight about driving?

During those tumultuous years, events pushed me onward. That might explain the gaps in my memory. I got through, like someone guided by GPS who passes through a city with little memory of the terrain.

As I read the physicians' notes, Dick's notes, and mine, my chest grew leaden, laden with such weighty cargo. Dick's wrenching message, "I can't avoid moving on to the horror," applied to me, as well.

CHAPTER 16

I Was Overpowered

The biblical Psalms are the "anatomy of the soul," declared John Calvin, the Protestant reformer. Taken as a whole, their language covers the full range of human experience, from wretchedness to exultation.

The psalm I'm most familiar with is the twenty-third, "The Lord is my shepherd," with its serene images of green pastures and still waters. I don't remember hearing any psalms of lamentation in church. They offer a stark contrast, with visions of floods, deep waters, engulfment, and drowning. Those songs surface during times of brokenness. They are "the shrill speeches" of the afflicted, "who suddenly discover that they are trapped and the water is rising," observes the theologian Walter Brueggemann.

≈

Years ago, I met a woman who told me she'd almost drowned while snorkeling off the Maui coast. She said, "I was choking, weak, disoriented, floundering up and down. I felt lost. Forsaken." That forsakenness can be heard in the psalmist's laments:

Psalm 69 - *"Save me, O God, for the waters are come into my soul. . . . I am come into deep waters, where the floods overflow me."*

Psalm 88 - *"Terrors have destroyed me. / All day long they surround me like a flood; / they have completely engulfed me."*

≈

During the rough middle phase of Dick's dementia, I came upon a reference to one of those songs of lament, Psalm 88. Curious, I pulled a copy of the Book of Psalms off our shelves. The words in that old deckle-edged volume stunned me. Psalm 88 is unrelentingly grim. There's no hope. Biblical scholars agree that it's unlike any other psalm. In the original Hebrew, the last word of Psalm 88 is *darkness*.

> *I am overwhelmed with troubles*
> *and my life draws near to death.*
> *I am counted among those who go down to the pit;*
> *I am like one without strength.*
> *I am set apart with the dead,*
> *like the slain who lie in the grave,*
> *whom you remember no more,*
> *who are cut off from your care.*
> *You have put me in the lowest pit,*
> *in darkest depths. . . .*
> *You have taken from me my closest friends*
> *and have made me repulsive to them.*
> *I am confined and cannot escape;*
> *my eyes are dim with grief. . . .*
> *Your wrath has swept over me;*
> *your terrors have destroyed me.*
> *All day long they surround me like a flood;*
> *they have completely engulfed me.*
> *You have taken from me friend and neighbor—*
> *darkness is my closest friend.*

≈

In an essay about Psalm 88, Brueggemann declares, "The movement of our life, if we are attentive, is the movement of orientation, disorientation and reorientation." The theologian Richard Rohr uses the terms *order*, *disorder*, and *reorder* and calls this "the wisdom pattern."

Life seems good, orderly, and reliable during times of orientation. We have a sense of wellbeing; we feel "at home." And so it was during the first twenty-five years that Dick and I shared.

We struggled to hang on to that stability when Dick began showing signs of dementia. But crises in 2005 swept away all that illusory normalcy. Near the end of that year, Dick wrote, "I was overpowered." It was as if a deluge had broken through a barrier, unmooring our lives.

The psalms of lament arise when we're swept away. These are the songs of disorientation, the "speeches of surprised dismay," says Brueggemann. How often had I told people that we "never expected" that Dick would be stricken with dementia? Nonetheless, it happened, and we were undone.

The psalmist's cries to God could have been uttered by my husband during those hellish years. No wonder I copied down Psalm 88. It was as if the psalmist spoke to us, murmuring, "I, too, have been here." *Here* was "in darkness, in the deeps." *Here* was in the trough of a towering wave. It engulfed us.

When people are drowning, they usually can't call for help. They swallow water, causing the voice box to spasm, cutting off air. They're rendered voiceless. It's called silent drowning.

When disorientation swallows us up, we're often stupefied: there's no flailing about, no shouting for help. Words fail.

At first, I had no words for how it felt to be in those depths. I used a clinical lexicon to cloak my fear—words like *symptoms* and *psychotropics* and *treatments*. The words I chose evaded the honest words that would voice my psychic reality.

What I did have were Dick's notes to me—cries of despair eked out in a ragged script. When he had written, "I can't avoid moving on to the horror," something in him grasped his plight. Brueggemann advises that we need to "embrace and recognize [the] real situation." Dick yielded to the disorientation—the horror—like the singer of Psalm 88.

It took longer for me to accept our new reality. "The movement of our life, if we are attentive . . ." *If we are attentive*: I am struck by Brueggemann's qualification.

To be attentive. To accept. That was what I had struggled to master.

≈

We sank to the depths but resurfaced, stripped of the facade of well-being. When we emerged from those rough waters, we found ourselves on a new shore.

In Dick's notes from 2005, I find several passages that move from disorientation to reorientation—from the maelstrom to quietude. They swing from primal howls of terror to paeans of love within a single page. They resemble a bobber in water: pulled down to the depths, then springing up. Down. Then up.

Reorientation is brought about by God's grace, according to Brueggemann. It's an unmerited gift. Grace was mysterious to me. It seemed like a conjuror's trick. But perhaps I didn't understand it. So I read more about grace. I learned that loving someone can be a form of grace. Like grace, profound love comes unbidden. It's a gift.

"Grace is love that cares and stoops and rescues," writes John Stott, a theologian. The grace of love brought Dick and me through the tempest and returned us to still waters.

CHAPTER 17

What Is, Is

"If they ask what Love is, / say: the sacrifice of will."
—Rumi, from *"The Inner Garment of Love"*

Life's tribulations will shatter us, observes Leon Wieseltier in his autobiography *Kaddish*. In those situations, "It is pointless to put up a fight." What, then, is one to do? Wieseltier concludes, "So there is only one thing to be done. Transformation must be met with transformation."

To do this, Wieseltier tells us we must "sink, so as to rise." We must stop flailing about and sink into the sea.

Dementia cast us into the sea during the most tempestuous phase. Nothing could save us. We sank to the sunless depths. Then our eyes adapted; we learned that we could see through that darkness.

Dick was the first to discern the pointlessness of fighting against dementia's plunder. In 2013, as he declined from moderate to severe dementia, Dick told me, "I love life as it is." He didn't simply declare "I love life." He concluded with the clear-eyed *as it is*. Dick also told me, "What is, is" more than once during that period.

The theologian Richard Rohr defines maturity as the ability "to accept that reality is what it is." *It is what it is. As it is. What is, is.*

Eventually, I accepted this wisdom, too. Then I could meet Dick's transformation with transformation.

≈

The golden egg in my wolverine dream signified transformation. During the middle stage of Dick's dementia, the shell of my resistance and anger began to crack.

Cracks appear on an eggshell's smooth surface and a living being emerges: an osprey or an owl, a siskin or a swan. We're captivated by such transformations. Children peer into a glass jar, waiting for a caterpillar to shed its skin, metamorphose into a chrysalis, and finally emerge as a butterfly. In myths and fairy tales, the beast or frog morphs into a prince, the weaver Arachne into a spider. Some stories feature humans who undergo a striking change, from Cinder-wench to Cinderella, from a guttersnipe to a lady in *Pygmalion*.

Advertisers show us before-and-after photos of overweight men and women turned svelte, transformed by a diet or exercise program. I used to pore over the "makeovers" pictured in *Teen* magazine. Just remove the glasses, change the hairdo, add a little makeup, and *Voila!*, the homely adolescent becomes a beauty.

Unlike the swift magic of a magician's wand, most transformations are slow and often difficult. The transformation of a caterpillar into a butterfly has been described as gruesome: the caterpillar digests itself. We only see the before-and-after photos, not the in-between ones, depicting the trials and failures, the discipline and discouragement.

The *before* part of our story was beautiful. In many ways, we'd led a charmed life. The *in-between* and *after* passages—the parts that were transformational—were slow and often difficult.

≈

Over our years together, I had this recurring dream: Dick and I are walking on a gravel road, he within sight but ahead of me. I thought the dream was about our age difference, about the likelihood that he'd die before I did. When we moved to the midpoint of his dementia, I realized that the dream might mean that he was leading me, always ahead.

At a reading I gave during National Alzheimer's Month, I mentioned that my husband had led me. A man in the audience questioned me: "You say, let them lead you—but where am I going?" He had given much of himself to caring for his elderly mother-in-law. Based on that experience, he concluded that people with dementia are "in a world that's totally out of this world. It's frightening. And we [loved ones/caregivers] are helpless."

His frustration and sorrow were palpable. Behind his comments, I detected a fundamental fear: the fear of losing control. He felt helpless to loosen dementia's hold on his mother-in-law. He wanted to change the situation, to take charge, to *do* something.

He wanted to lead, not follow. *Where am I going?* He feared following his mother-in-law into a "world out of this world," like Alice in her Wonderland. Later, I realized that it might have reassured him to know that following the deeply forgetful into their world doesn't mean we take up residence there.

The caregiver is "a messenger between worlds." And in that "dance between these worlds, the person with forgetfulness leads, and you, the helper, follow," observe Nader Robert Shabahangi and Bogna Szymkiewicz, psychotherapists.

Some prefer not to enter that uncanny land. They cling to the illusion that they can and should control the narrative as it unspools. Because Dick was forty-one when I met him—mature and very much himself—I knew I couldn't control or change him, nor did I try.

Attempts to force someone with dementia to conform to our reality probably won't succeed, anyway. Rather, we should seek to "enter in the logic, landscape, and culture" of people with dementia, to "try to be where they are," concludes the author Gisela Webb.

To "be where they are," one needs to decipher the actions of the person who has dementia, because often he or she cannot say, cannot explain. Just as we read a temperature, a musical score, or the weather, we learn to read a loved one. How apt that I would need to read my husband during his dementia, since we both were such avid readers.

≈

Years ago, I declared that my epitaph should be, *Not to expect too much; not to expect too little*. The equipoise of that maxim appealed to me: one foot balanced on either side of a teeter-totter's fulcrum. It served me well through the uncertainties of Dick's dementia.

Not to expect too little: Rather than dwelling on Dick's deficits, I focused on his remaining strengths. I expected that he would remain fundamentally himself. I expected that even as he drifted away, we still could find one another. I expected that our love would anchor us.

Not to expect too much: To expect too much is to have "a sentimental view of life, and this is a softness that ends in bitterness," avers the novelist Flannery O'Connor. I shared O'Connor's cautious stance—and my life with Dick did not end in bitterness.

I realized the wisdom of not expecting too much. When I arrived home after work, it was best not to bear expectations as to the state Dick might be in. Dick could be amiable or agitated; he could be lucid or delusional; he could be ravenous or refuse to eat. If I'd expected to see a contented man but found him angered, I'd have been dismayed. If I'd steeled myself for an outburst, he might have delighted me with his greeting: "Hello, my beautiful sunshine!"

Not-to-expect is to accept what is, which enabled me to meet my husband where he was and to see him as he was.

≈

Acceptance is not weakness. It's tough-minded and undaunted. Acceptance makes peace with what is, instead of denying or resisting it. In our case, it meant confronting the actualities of dementia—but it didn't mean giving up.

I needed to accept that I couldn't rescue Dick from the dementia. But I could keep reinforcing *him*, the self-that-remained.

≈

I once worked in a candle factory. One day, an irritable supervisor pointed out a trait of mine. After the molten wax had set, I removed the candles from metal forms and prepared them for packaging. As I carefully wiped bits of wax from a candle, she barked, "Don't do that with such affection!"

It struck me then—it still strikes me fifty years later—how my supervisor's intended insult was remarkably perceptive. My absorption in the task at hand annoyed her. She demanded briskness, not careful attention. But I could do my work no other way, so I quit the job.

≈

I wanted to attend to Dick with such affection. The Latin root of *attend* means "to stretch toward." I wanted to meet my husband wherever he was: resting quietly with eyes closed, or seeing visions of invisible birds, or singing a familiar tune, or uttering sentences strewn with his delightful coinages, such as *sunion* and *sighla*.

I listened with curiosity, fascinated by how my husband's mind worked. I couldn't attempt to decipher what he said or did unless I was paying close attention. In some ways, my noticing was similar to an artist's or scientist's careful observations. I was attentive, for I was enthralled.

The year before he died, Dick told me, "You listen carefully."

≈

Years later, I was moved by Arthur Kleinman's comments on caregiving. Kleinman, a physician and anthropologist, describes caregiving as a moral practice and "a practice of empathic imagination." He says that caregiving "makes caregivers, and at times even the care-receivers, more present and thereby fully human."

I supported Dick's efforts to remain present by caring for him with affection and attention. By meeting transformation with transformation, my empathic imagination was enlarged. I became more fully human.

PART 4

Sustaining, Unselfing, Growing

CHAPTER 18

I Appreciate You Doing This

As we readied for his bath, Dick struggled to remove his socks. I bent down to help him. I couldn't slip off his socks with ease. I tugged and yanked, forcing them over the angles, the oddness, of the foot.

I'd already helped him take off his turtleneck and tee-shirt, his jeans and briefs. He stood before me, naked. We were used to it. Years ago—years before the onset of my husband's dementia—we'd strip off our clothes on hot summer afternoons, then take turns under the solar shower on the deck. The south-facing deck captured the sun's light; woods fringed the eastern edge. Aspen leaves revealed their pale underbellies as breezes set leaves quivering and teased our pale flesh dry. We were not shy. At ease in our bodies, we took delight in one another.

Years ago, I'd slide under the bedcovers warmed by Dick's warmth, fit my body next to his, kiss his back and neck and mouth, then fall asleep in his embrace. Some nights his kisses would slowly stir me from deep sleep. Like two dream animals, we'd clasp one another and make blind love in the dark. Then I'd open my eyes to see him: carnal, mortal, beautiful.

From the moment I met him years ago, I was taken with him. *Taken* in the sense of being attracted and enchanted. Like taking a deep breath of air, I'd take him in: welcoming him into my body.

≈

We inhabited our marriage. It was our dwelling place for more than forty years. As much as our marriage was about love, it also was about a shared physicality. We grew so accustomed to working together that there would be no need for talk; we'd read one another's body language.

Because of that familiarity and ease, as Dick's disease progressed, I was comfortable with the more intimate caregiving tasks—the bathing, clothing, and feeding, and the assistance with toileting. He entrusted his body to me.

When dementia took him, our carnal pleasures became just an arousing memory for me. And for him? As he descended deeper into dementia, his memories of our ardor receded but didn't vanish altogether. As we cuddled in his narrow bed at the assisted living home, he told me, "Two is happy," and asked, "Could I hold you for a couple of hours?" Once, when I climbed into his bed to snuggle, he asked, "Can we do naughty things?"

During his remaining years, washing his naked body would elicit the deepest of physical intimacies, skin against skin. When we are intimate, we allow ourselves to touch and be touched by the other. In intimacy, we let the other in. Even in his last days, he'd often take me in with his eyes, with a love that was palpable. It felt as if he'd touched me.

≈

As Dick's dementia progressed, our intense conversations and physical passions fell away. And what remained? The pleasure and comfort of touch. We'd hold hands. I'd stroke his hair and rub his back. I'd drape an arm across his sleeping body or wrap both arms around him in a hug. With my index finger, I'd trace his temples, nose, and cheekbones, the shape of his mouth. I would kiss his eyelids as he rested. "You have a soft way of doing," he told me.

During the final years of his life, touch became an essential means of communication. In an article about the care of persons with dementia, the author Rebecca Mead observes that our society prizes cognition "at the expense of other essential human qualities: sensuality, pleasure, intimacy. For people who can no longer think clearly, a life of small sensory pleasures is a considerable achievement."

This is not how our society usually defines achievement, but I take it to mean the attainment of satisfaction or happiness. How suitable, given that the Latin root of *attain* is *tangere,* "to touch."

IN THE EVENING, WE'LL DANCE

≈

I bathed Dick twice a week while he still lived at home—more than a hundred times a year, for more than eight years. Once the bathwater was drawn, I rested a hand between his shoulder blades to guide him as he stepped into the tub. I held onto his left arm—a gesture, really, as he needed no assistance. He was wiry.

Sometimes, I'd praise him: "My strong husband!" He'd respond by flexing his right arm, proudly pointing out the firm bicep. He did this with friends and even strangers, asking them if they wanted to feel his muscles. Some were shy, some taken aback, while others were game. They'd laugh, feel his bicep, and affirm that, yes, he still was strong.

He *was* strong. But his vigor frightened me at times. As his memory diminished, it was possible that someday he might not recognize me. Would he fight against the stranger I'd become? And might his hardy body keep him alive until the last, vegetative stage? How could I bear it?

Supported by his strong arms and lean legs, he lowered himself into the tub with ease. I lathered up a washcloth and instructed him to scrub his face, including the beard and mustache. He closed his eyes as he rubbed his face with the cloth. Each time I watched him do this I would admire the curve of his eyelids beneath his well-formed brow. High cheekbones further defined his large hazel eyes. Such a beautiful man.

"Oh, no!" exclaimed a friend when I told her that Dick had dementia. "He's such a beautiful man." By "beautiful" she probably was referring to his kindness. (Or did she mean his charm? His integrity? I should have asked.) But he *was* beautiful to look at.

≈

The scant, still-dark hair on his chest formed a nimbus around the nipples, which I would kiss. He washed his chest, then I directed him to scrub his arms and armpits. He did so, clumsily. He tried to follow my instructions, but his hands were no longer deft.

Sometimes he looked up at me and declared, "You're my wife." Or asked, "Are we married?" I suppose it was the physical intimacy that prompted this. The space islanded us, too: the small room, warmed by the moist heat of the bathwater. As he shifted his weight in the tub, the tiled walls amplified the lapping of the water.

I reminded him, "Wash your tummy, too." Once, he looked down at his stomach, grown a little flabby, and said, "I only have *one* tummy, not two," then grinned up at me. He loved homophones. "Watch out for deer," he cautioned when I'd drive at night. "And there's a dear right here, next to me," he'd add. It pleased him. It pleased me.

Step-by-step, we made our way through each bath-time. An abrupt or unexpected move might frighten him, so, as I rose to wash his back, I'd tell him, "Now I'll wash your neck and your back." I'd tuck my hand under his chin to lift it. Then I scrubbed his neck. Next, I'd bend down to wash Dick's long freckled back. His shoulders were curved, rounded by years hunched over a keyboard, writing. But that was only part of it. The burden of dementia pressed down on him: his rounded shoulders, his plodding steps, his downcast gaze.

Years before, during the early stages of Dick's disease, I saw a husband and wife in a local pharmacy. He trailed behind her, holding her hand and moving slowly, uncertainly, in her wake. I realized that I'd just seen a vision of our future, but I closed my mind to it.

≈

I paused to wring out the washcloth before rinsing his back. Then I asked him to clean his lower body. He washed his genitals gingerly. Next, the thighs, lower legs, and feet. Sometimes he hesitated, as if pondering what a thigh might be. He reached down, rubbing randomly on the left calf, his thigh. Then stopped. "Now the right," I reminded him.

I asked him if he wanted me to wash his feet. He had broad feet with rounded toes that curled downward, as if frightened. His feet seemed an anomaly, the chubby terminus of such an angular body.

His answer was always yes. So I'd lean over the tub and wedge the washcloth between his toes, clamped tightly one to the other. As I rubbed each foot, sometimes he'd say, "I appreciate you doing this."

I wonder why he said that at that very moment. What is it about foot washing that evoked his response? It begins with the bare foot, which is a sign of humility in many cultures. The humble Francis, a Catholic saint, went unshod. People remove their shoes when entering holy places, such as mosques or Hindu temples.

Touching or washing another person's feet can be a sign of humility, hospitality, service, or reverence. Hindus show respect for elders by touching their bare feet in a salutation called *Charanasparsha* (Sanskrit for *touching the feet*). The physician and author Atul Gawande describes this practice. His grandfather lived in a village in India, where "he was revered—not in spite of his age but because of it. . . . When young people came into his home, they bowed and touched his feet in supplication."

Many Christian denominations observe foot washing rites, called Maundy. They are following the example of Jesus, as recounted in the Gospel of John. An honored person, Jesus, offers to wash the feet of his apostles as a sign of servanthood and solidarity. In *Christ Washing the Feet of the Apostles*, a painting by Meister des Hausbuches, Jesus is depicted kneeling by a basin of water, a plain white towel tied around his waist, one of his bare feet peeking out awkwardly from beneath his black robe.

The apostle before whom he kneels has a hand on Christ's arm, as if to stop him. This probably is Simon Peter, who did not want to accept Christ's gift. Jesus looks up at Simon Peter, his hand raised, index finger pointing. Is it a gesture of instruction, or is it a gesture of command?

Servants performed foot washing to welcome guests into a home, but Simon Peter viewed Christ as his master. "Jesus has to insist on being the servant lover," observes the Catholic scholar Richard Rohr. "It is hard to receive undeserved love from another. We want to think we have earned any love that we get by our worthiness." A few of the other apostles portrayed in the painting also seem resistant. Most close their eyes in prayer, while a few watch in wonder.

I watched in wonder as Dick's trusted physician, Dr. Goodall, spread a white towel under my husband's feet, knelt before him, and proceeded to clip Dick's toenails. This gesture transformed a routine examination. The grey clinic room suddenly seemed a sacred space. As in des Hausbuches' painting, the respected central figure bowed down, not as a supplicant, but as one conferring a loving gift. Unlike Simon Peter, Dick sat quietly to receive it.

≈

Following the foot washing, my final task was to shampoo my husband's hair—silver, thinning on top, but still remarkably thick for an eighty-one-year-old. First, I'd warn him that I needed to use the shower head to wash his hair. Showers seemed to frighten him. Before each bath, I'd ask him, "Would you like to take a shower or a bath?" I wanted him to have choices. He never chose a shower. Perhaps the sudden, forceful downpour of water startled him.

I slowly turned on the shower to dampen his hair, then lathered up the shampoo. I rubbed his scalp with my fingertips. When I was a child, I enjoyed it when my mother did this for me, so I lingered over the task with a vicarious pleasure.

This quiet interlude ended with a command: "Eyes shut. Mouth shut. Rinse." He squeezed his eyes tightly and clamped his mouth into a thin line. I rinsed off the suds, inhaling a last citrusy whiff of the shampoo. Then I handed a towel to him so that he could dry his face and open his eyes.

It was time to get out of the tub. I reminded him to hold on to the grab bar and get his feet under himself. He popped up and gingerly lifted one long, thin leg out of the tub, then the other. Dry ground. Without the sounds of water, the room suddenly grew still.

After his bath, he'd often ask me, "Is this home?" I wondered what prompted this. Lacking memory, he already was adrift in time. Had enclosure in this warm, watery world made him feel adrift in space, as well?

"Yes," I reassured him. "This is home."

He stood patiently as I toweled him off, top to bottom. After drying his feet, I rose. We faced one another. He turned his gentle gaze downward, looked me in the eyes, and kissed me.

CHAPTER 19
There's So Much to Say, but I'm Not Capable

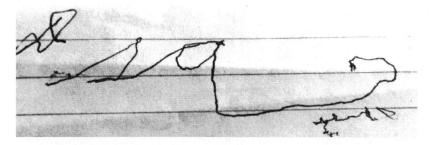

Three months before his death, Dick wrote this and then said, "Resistance." He formed the letter *D* in the same flamboyant cursive he used when writing his name. The *D* is followed by a gap, then what appear to be the letters *sa*. The *a* trails downward, swings upward, and ends with a tail, a tassel—or a lash. Beneath, an agitated scribble. *More to say. No way to say it.*

≈

After his death, I dreamed that Dick was next to me in bed. I turned over and there he was, facing me. He wore beige pajamas covered with lettering: black letters printed in straight lines, written in an angular, urgent script. When I woke, I tried to recall some of the sentences but could not. I might not have been able to read them.

≈

Writing anchors words, shapes sounds into text. Both *text* and *textile* come from the Latin root, *texere*, to weave. To write is to weave a nest of words. Dick was a writer—of articles, news reports, books, letters. We were immersed in language, our lives replete with repartee, abounding in dialogue about our thoughts, our reading, our writing.

Then his word nest unraveled. There's a word for that: *agraphia*, the loss of the capacity to communicate through writing. The agraphia progressed gradually, as did his *alexia*, an inability to understand written words. Both are caused by damage to the brain.

At first, he'd forget what he'd just read, so his books were littered with slips of paper and pencilled markings. Then he lost interest in books altogether: the volumes arrayed along the north wall of our log house, stacked the length of the south window ledge, heaped beneath his desk, crammed into the bookshelves by our bed. He declared, "We have enough books."

On the evening before a camping trip with his son, Joe, Dick announced that he wasn't bringing any books with him. He said, "Nature will be my book."

≈

Dick continued to use his considerable vocabulary correctly, despite his struggles with language. He no longer knew what day, month, or year it was, but he remained a logophile, a lover of words. He described our dog Phoenix as *rambunctious* and *precocious*, with *lustrous* fur.

In 2012—one year before I had to move him to a facility—I suggested that he be more parsimonious with the milk, to save room for his dinner. He replied, "In plain language, that means stingy." En route home following a visit with relatives, he said, "I surmise we'll get home soon." On another trip, we drove by a casino, its parking lot filled with cars. I noted that people were indoors gambling on such a sunny afternoon. "That's decadent," said Dick.

Shortly before his death, an aide at Oak Hill apologized to Dick for talking a lot. He reassured her, "At least you weren't pontificating."

In their guide to Alzheimer's, the psychiatrists Leonard Heston and June A. White note, "A verbally fluent person can continue to produce grammatically correct sentences using a large vocabulary despite a moderately advanced dementia." It took several years for Dick to be diagnosed with dementia because he aced language-based tests. In 2000, he had an interview with a neurologist. She asked him to list words beginning with the letter *S*. Dick quickly recalled numerous words, doubling the number of words that would mark the usual cut-off. She determined that he didn't have pre-Alzheimer's.

Five years later, when Dick was discharged from his first stay in a geriatric psychiatric ward, I asked the staff, "Is it Alzheimer's?" They thought not, due to his lexical fluency.

≈

We faced one another on opposite sides of our bed when we made it each morning. Sometimes, we'd rhyme words, volleying them across the width of the bed: *Scent. Bent. Dent. Lament. Augment.* One morning, I began with *out. Spout. Shout. Doubt. Bout.* Back and forth we went, until he came up with *Terre Haute.* End game. As his dementia progressed, he'd still play with words. Rhyming *late* and *bait*, Dick added, "*Sate*. That's when you've had enough."

After he'd moved to Oak Hill, we'd often snuggle together in his bed during my visits. I gathered in his warmth, one arm flung across his chest or belly, mouth and chin pressed into his shoulder. One afternoon, I whispered to him, "I love to cuddle you."

He replied, "Cuddle, snuggle, subtle." I laughed with delight at *subtle*, with its slant rhyme.

≈

Dick also prolonged his ability to communicate by making up words. As he gradually lost the names of things, he compensated with delightful coinages.

His knuckles became *nimnits*. He sang to me, then informed me that his song was a *hermatation*. He told me about *hegatones* and *sunions*.

He said, "Last time I went to *sayshone-sayshone*. I said two words."

"What two words did you say?" I asked, hoping to clarify.

"Sun shine," he replied, then began to sing, "You Are My Sunshine."

At times, gestures would suffice for the absent word. When we'd go on a car ride, he'd usually say, "Watch out for deer." One day, he didn't say that. Instead, he asked, "What's the long thing?" He traced a horizontal oval with his hand.

"Thing?"

"Yes."

"An animal?"

"Yes."

I guessed a deer, based on the graceful way he moved his hand.

"Yes, deer."

≈

> *"Humor was another of the soul's weapons in the fight for self-preservation."*
> —Viktor Frankl, *Man's Search for Meaning*

Dick preserved his sense of self—and a central part of that self was wit. His sense of humor ranged octaves, ascending the scales from crude to corny to clever, from risqué to irreverent. Sometimes the jests were scatological. He noted that a rabbit had left its "calling cards" under the shrubbery; he called the dog's circular paths in the snow "poop loops."

In 1998, the year his memory loss became apparent, Dick wrote "Misc. Oddments" on the cover of a small notebook. It contained his reading notes and a few news clippings, including this:

LOST: SMALL, UGLY PONTOON BOAT ON BALL CLUB LAKE.

Dick seldom told jokes. Instead, he poked fun. In 2001, he'd clipped out a newspaper ad for Memorial Day. Under a sketch of the red-white-and-blue, the text advertised

Patriotic Flags
Starting At 59¢
Under which he'd neatly penciled in:
UNPATRIOTIC FLAGS - 49¢

Even as his dementia progressed, the humor remained. Humor has the ability not only to express the amusing or comical, but also the incongruous or absurd. He'd use humor like a finger-poke, to jab at human folly or pretense. And, always, his humor was quick.

Just two years before Dick's death, his psychiatrist said to him, "You look very calm. Would you agree?"

My husband replied, "I don't know. I can't see myself."

≈

Dick moved from lucidity to incoherence, from humor or insight to a frustrated jumble of word-sounds.

"I got all jammed up here," he said, after trailing off at the beginning of a sentence.

I asked him "What did? Your words?"

"Yes. But it's not too bad."

He glanced at his wrist and told me, "I need to look at my mirror." I asked him if he meant his watch. "Yes. I said that wrong."

His syntax always was correct, but nouns often seemed to elude him. One day, he told me he'd seen some *licky dobers*. He told me about *ughitables*. He declared, "Last night I went into the *jungersill*."

However, the word he most often used when a noun escaped his memory was *sunshine:* "Army, navy, and . . . sunshine."

≈

Early in his dementia, Dick left this note for me: "There's so much to say, but I'm not capable."

He recognized that his communication skills—reading, writing, and speaking—were waning. It was analogous to the deteriorating communication between neurons in his brain.

The brain's ability to send and receive messages declines in neurodegenerative diseases such as dementia. The synapses, axons, and, ultimately, the nerve cells themselves deteriorate and die. When neurons lose their function, they no longer transmit impulses. They can't communicate. First there's static on the line, and then the signal fails.

"The inability to speak the correct words or to pronounce words correctly or to speak many words at all does not mean that the person involved has vanished," argues the neuropsychologist Steven Sabat. Persons with dementia are still there, although the disease often renders them unable to articulate their thoughts intelligibly.

On occasion, I would join Dick at Oak Hill for dinner with the other residents, many of whom also had dementia. Once, Dick stopped eating, leaned over to me, and said, "Some people have a hard time talking with people who have lost their—[long pause]—claver."

Whether or not persons with dementia can still communicate clearly, they will benefit from "nonjudgmental people and the non-anxious presence of others." They "need to be listened to and heard," advises Sabat.

≈

Dick observed quietly when friends and I were engaged in a lively conversation. Sometimes, he'd interject: "Look at me! Listen to me!" We'd all fall silent. He'd pause. Now what? Then, he'd recite, "When I was a windy boy and a bit," or sing "You Are My Sunshine," or declare how much he loved me.

I learned to pause, listen, and be present to Dick. Sabat recommends active listening: giving the person our focused attention and asking questions when what is said is unclear. These actions signal to persons with dementia that we are interested in them and want to communicate with them. Rather than the detached, head-nodding, "uh-huh" form of listening, the active listener is engaged.

A friend told me, "You always focused your attention on listening to what Dick had to say." She observed that often people are so busy running their own stories in their heads and thinking about what they'll do next, that they don't really listen to what the other person has to say. And they may assume that people with dementia have nothing to say, so they don't listen.

She said that it was helpful to witness the relationship between Dick and me: "Probably the only thing that saved me from doing these things is that I had you as a model. So my interactions with Dick were profound for me in their own way. I wasn't always certain of what the conversation was about, but it seemed secondary to just being together. I never felt like I was wasting my time."

Those acts of truly listening helped to sustain the relationship between Dick and me. I remained engaged and curious. I wanted to listen. I wanted to learn from the remarkable story that was unfolding before me. And I didn't want it to end.

≈

Less than a year before his death, Dick rested in bed, "typing" on the bedspread. He paused to scribble a note in the air above him. He remained a writer.

The Old English word for *write* means to form letters by carving. It reminds me of the Germanic runes, letters carved into bone and stone. In Norse mythology, the god Odin sacrificed himself to gain the runes. As he hung from Yggdrasil, the cosmic tree at the center of the universe, the runes appeared at his feet. He learned to decipher them and then "each word led me on to another word."

Less than a year before Dick's death, one word led to another in a note to me. He wrote the words—some sure, some uncertain—in blue ink on coarse paper in an effortful, uneven script. But the message was clear.

CHAPTER 20

Don't Forget the Singing

"Music begins where language ends."
—Henry Russell Cleveland, essayist

Beyond love and language, music sustained us. The Latin root of *sustain* means *to hold up*. *To sustain* is to bear a weight without breaking, falling, or sinking. *To sustain* also refers to sustenance, the nourishment of spirit, life, and health. While we bore the load of Dick's dementia, music sustained us, enlivening our minds and feeding our souls.

In music, a *sustain* is a steady state of sound. When I practiced the piano as a child, I loved to use the sustain pedal, even when the score didn't call for it. The sound seemed to envelop me. The pedal prolonged the vibration of the strings after I let up on the keys. It also prolonged the waning of the sound as it faded into silence.

≈

The part of the brain that responds to music is the last to atrophy and succumb to dementia. Even when the dementia is advanced, music still has a therapeutic role, since "musical perception, musical sensibility, musical emotion, and musical memory can survive long after other forms of memory have disappeared," according to the neurologist Oliver Sacks.

Through music, people with dementia seem to temporarily transcend the disease. "There are many levels at which music can call to people, enter them, alter them," asserts Sacks. Music can calm, focus, anchor, and engage persons who have dementia. I witnessed those effects in Dick and others.

161

The role of music in human life began early in our evolution. Unearthed flutes, the earliest known musical instruments, were fashioned more than 40,000-50,000 years ago. They were shaped from a cave bear's femur, a vulture's wing bone, bones of the mute swan, and the wooly mammoth's ivory. With a human's breath, the bones came alive with song.

There are three schools of thought about when music arose in the evolutionary development of humans, explains Sacks. Some scientists argue that humans developed language before music. Others believe that they arose simultaneously, while the third camp thinks that music preceded language. Darwin argued for the latter. A century before Darwin, the philosopher Jean-Jacques Rousseau invented the term *protomusilanguage* for his theory that ancestral humans first communicated by singing.

Any music lover will attest to the powerful emotional effect a song can have. "Ultimately, music is the communication of emotion, the most fundamental form of communication," observes the anthropologist Robin Dunbar. "The deeply emotional stirrings generated by music suggest to me that music has very ancient origins, long predating the evolution of language."

≈

When Dick still lived at home, he began most days joyfully, with several renditions of "You Are My Sunshine," dedicated to Phoenix and me. He once woke up singing the chorus of "Itsy Bitsy Teenie Weenie Yellow Polka Dot Bikini." I told him it was a very silly song. He replied, "There's room for silly songs, too."

Songs and music were threaded throughout our days. As I was about to leave for work one morning, Dick held my hands, looked into my eyes, and sang, "I'll Be Loving You Always." When we walked by the light of a full moon, he crooned, "Full Moon and Empty Arms"—only he adapted the lyrics, singing "Full moon and full arms."

One evening in November of 2011, I chronicled the chores we'd completed that day. I reminded Dick that we'd accomplished a lot:

We'd washed four loads of clothes, harvested some carrots, and made a big pot of split pea soup. Dick said, "Don't forget the singing!"

≈

Dick added "Onward, Christian Soldiers" and "The Battle Hymn of the Republic" to his repertoire during the later stages of his dementia. Harkening back to music learned in one's early life, such as hymns, touches the "enduring selves" of persons with dementia. One of the last parts of the brain to atrophy, the medial prefrontal cortex, "links memory, music, and emotion," according to the bioethicist Stephen G. Post.

I told Dick that I disliked the martial lyrics of those hymns. But when he began singing, I'd join in. Once, after we'd rendered a few bars of "Onward, Christian Soldiers," he sang it by himself. When he got to "With the cross of Jesus, going on before," he substituted his own words: "Phoenix and his mittens, going on before." After much laughter, I joined him. Then he soloed, changing the same line—only this time it was, "Looking on the bright side, which they never do." Another version: "With the love of Jesus, going on before. "

When we sang "The Battle Hymn," I asked him what the truth was in the refrain, "His truth is marching on."

"Love," was Dick's reply.

≈

I'd ask Dick what music he wanted to hear when we were at home or riding in the car, as well as when he was in a psychiatric ward or the assisted living home. We shared a love for many musical genres, but most often, he would request jazz: *Kind of Blue* by Miles Davis, *Monk's Dream* by Thelonious Monk, and ballads by John Coltrane and Paul Desmond. He liked Paul Simon's music, Tony Bennett's *Duets*, the *Blue* album by Joni Mitchell, the Celtic harmonies of Anúna, the Cuban rhythms of the Buena Vista Social Club, as well as the music of Bach, Vivaldi, Handel, and Mozart, among others.

As I drove home from Oak Hill after visits with Dick, I often played the music of Dave Matthews Band. I turned up the volume and sang along. I'd spent hours with the aged and dying, so I needed the band's joy, their zest, their strong beat and complex sound. I sang along with their lyrics to remind myself that "life is short but sweet, for certain" and to "celebrate, we will." It was my way of declaring, "I'm still alive!"

"You can't sing and cry, you just can't." This truth was conveyed to the poet Heather Christle by a church sexton.

≈

Early in our relationship, Dick told me that he couldn't sing. I disagreed, for I'd heard him sing some complex tunes. He just needed ear training in order to match a pitch. I sang a note, held it, and waited for him to join me. He struggled, his baritone voice wandering above and below the pitch I sang to him. He quickly grew impatient with the exercise.

But when he developed dementia, he sang a lot—confidently and in tune. I wondered about the change. Perhaps it was because the dementia made him less self-conscious. His confidence also may have been due to his years of humming, when he "sang" tunes with his lips closed.

Dick often hummed. In fact, our friend Suzann Nelson recalled a time when he worked with her at the Northern Minnesota Citizens League. Dick served as a researcher and writer. She said that Dick arrived in the office "whistling or humming" and noted that "it is hard to remain crabby when co-workers are humming."

People throughout the world hum, and "many more people hum than sing," according to the ethnomusicologist Joseph Jordania. He observes that "humming is predominantly connected to positive feelings and attitudes." It's a sign of contentment. Jordania adds, "Humming (and singing) can also calm an anxious person and relax a troubled mind."

Humming has another function among social animals, which is to create a feeling of safety. When the group hums, it's called "contact calling." On the other hand, silence signals danger.

Years ago, a humming sound broke the silence of a spring afternoon for Dick and me. We'd gone on a bike ride, making our way over a worn path through the hayfield to the gravel road in front of our log

IN THE EVENING, WE'LL DANCE

house. We headed west, past the last homestead on our dead-end road. The road narrowed, dipped into a swampy area, then grew hummocky. It ended in a stand of balsam and poplar.

When we reached the swamp, we heard a low, humming sound. It continued as we pedaled uphill, then faded away. Neither of us could identify it. It wasn't the song of frogs or toads, or any bird. I researched this mysterious sound when we returned home. I learned that it probably was the humming of bear cubs. Black bears roamed our woods; we'd see them quite often. Once, we'd witnessed a female and her three cubs ambling across that very stretch of road.

I learned that the vocalization cubs produce resembles a "sustained monotonous hum or buzz" and is "clearly audible at some distance from the den," according to a study by the biologists Gustav Peters, Megan Owen, and Lynn Rogers. Researchers have observed that cubs hum while they are on their own for its "relaxing, soothing effect." As in humans, humming in bears "signals comfort or contentment."

Jordania describes human humming as "singing in [the] head." It's created by our breath, as the air moves and resonates through passages in the head and throat. A hum might be one of the first sounds we hear. Hearing is the earliest of the five senses to develop; while they're still in the womb, babies can hear their mother's heart beat and her lungs fill with air. They can hear her voice as she speaks and sings. Imagine how a lullaby would sound to a fetus deep inside the mother's body, inside a fluid-filled amniotic sac. Might it resemble a hum?

≈

A year before he died, a small stroke left Dick listing markedly to one side, unable to focus his eyes or speak. I talked to him, but he couldn't respond. So I began to sing. He looked me in the eyes, then joined me. As we sang, we breathed together.

If I were in a room with you, my breath would carry these words to your ears. My words would emerge from the cave of my body—from the lungs in my chest, through the narrow passage of my throat and the cavities of mouth and sinuses. "The human voice comes from inside

165

the human organism which provides the voice's resonances. . . . Sound pours into the hearer," notes the philosopher Walter Ong in his discussion of the interiority of sound.

≈

I'm most aware of my breathing when singing in a chorus. Taking a deep breath helps produce a full tone and carries the tune through until the next breath mark—those little apostrophes that hover above the musical staff. Sometimes, the score calls for the chorus to hum, mouths closed. When I hum, my breath moves through the boney cavities of my head and resonates. I'm reminded of the *Om* chanted during meditation, the hum of *M* resonating within.

Music and song—always part of our lives—took on an even greater significance during the years of Dick's dementia. When I had to move him to the assisted living home, I gathered a stack of music books—*Everybody's Favorite Folk Songs*, Christmas carols, hymns, collections of "best songs"—and stored them in his room. We'd sit side by side and I'd sing to him from one of those books. He'd often join me, humming when he couldn't remember the lyrics, because Dick could no longer read. We'd breathe in. Then the sounds of song, buoyed by our breath, would float out into his room.

≈

The poet Anne Carson writes of "the ancient struggle of breath against death." During the last night of Dick's life, I lay next to him and quietly sang to him. The gentle, soothing sounds resembled a lullaby. When I'd cease singing, the room filled with his ragged breath.

One of the names for that struggle is *air hunger*. He breathed heavily, as though he craved air but could not get enough. This noisy breathing is called a "death rattle."

As the night wore on, the rattling was joined by *rales*—a crackling sound made by splashing in his lungs as they began filling with fluid, rather than air. The person feels as if he is suffocating.

Near the end, his gasps for air were followed by a cessation in breathing. Then another gasp, as if he were about to take a long dive under water. His breathing resembled the finale of Beethoven's 5th symphony: A thunderous chord. Then silence. "It's finished," the listener thinks. Suddenly, another chord and another, each jarring chord broken by a pause.

Dick's breathing became so labored that I got up from his bed and called the aide. I asked her to give him some morphine. As she sat by his bedside with the needle in hand, he stopped breathing. She timed the quiet interlude. One minute. He gasped for air. Then two minutes of silence. He gasped again.

Then silence. Silence. Silence.

CHAPTER 21

This Crown Is Heavy

I took this photo of my husband shortly before his eighty-third birthday, his last, in April of 2015. My friend Elizabeth says it reminds her of an icon. The word *icon* means *image* and is used to refer to sacred artworks in which religious figures—saints, Jesus, the Virgin Mary—are portrayed.

Much of the religious art with which I'm familiar brings "the sacred into our world," as Wendy Beckett, an art historian, puts it. Such art "domesticates the sacred" in richly detailed canvases—winged angels and haloed saints appear amidst a jumble of hillside flora, walled cities, potentates and peasants.

Icons move the viewer in the opposite direction, from this world into the world of the sacred. An icon often contains only one figure. The focus is on the visage, which is emphasized by a halo behind the head. The saintly figures depicted usually have either a stern or serene demeanor. They often face the viewer with an expression that's startlingly direct, yet enigmatic. They've had a revelation that can't be put into words.

It is said that contemplation of an icon can serve as a window to the sacred. I studied those iconic faces, their air of being both here and not here. I think that sense of movement, from this world to a sacred realm, from the mundane to the mysterious, might be why Elizabeth compared the portrait of my husband to an icon. It speaks to her and to me of both corporeality and spirit. I wonder if my husband, like the figures in icons, had experienced something ineffable.

Each night before I go to bed, I pause before this photograph. The left half of his face is in shadow, the right lit by late afternoon sunlight streaming in through a window. Two halves: Light and dark. Life and death.

Barely touching the cool glass with my index finger, I trace his brow, his eyelids, the long nose, the cheekbones, the chin. I linger at the mouth, slightly curved, content. As I run my finger across the lips, I feel the bristle of his beard on my body. I trace my husband's image to evoke his presence as I grapple with his absence.

≈

For more than a decade of Dick's illness, I held pairs of antithetical concepts in a deft balance. The clean line between *this* and *that* blurs when living with dementia. During the final few years of his life, my husband retained his selfhood, but he also entered transitory states of unselfing. He was both himself and self-less, both present and absent, both here and away. When Dick was away, he was still here; he just wasn't present to me in the usual sense. At first, I feared dementia's awayness until I learned to swing on the pendulum of *away / here, absent / present, unselfed / self*. I learned to feel his presence in the absences.

≈

In the vivid dream I'd entered into my journal before I married Dick, we spoke koan-like vows: "*I marry this no-one.*" Those words were an unraveled riddle that I'd set aside, then forgotten. The *no-one* of our vows came to mind during Dick's moments of unselfing.

Unself is a curious word. It's rarely used. Spellcheck doesn't recognize it. Although definitions of *unself* appear when I google it, some dictionaries, including mine, omit it. However, I do find columns of words beginning with the prefix *un-*. Many are adjectives describing a state of negation, with *un-* signifying *not*: unaware, uncharted, unknown. However, the *un-* of *unself* denotes action. It's a prefix that indicates alteration, removal, reversal, or release. Some *un-* verbs, such as *undo* and *unravel*, hint at the fears that unselfing can engender.

To unself sounds ominous, like plummeting into the void of a dreamless sleep. It seems like a death. In a way, it is. Many spiritual traditions speak of a "dying to the self." It's a reminder that we are more than our ego-selves.

The psychiatrist Carl Jung envisioned the entirety of the self as a circle, at the center of which, like the axle on a wheel, stands the sturdy dot of ego. The ego is an expression of the self, or, as Jung explains, "the visibility of the self." But the self is more than ego. The totality of the self, says Jung, is "the great secret which has to be worked out."

The word *ego* literally means *I* in Latin. Buddhists refer to *I* as "the mark of self." The ego shapes and organizes a child's personal identity, distinguishing *I* from *Other*. Our ego-selves serve us in everyday life, in our relational identities (parent, sibling, spouse); professional capacities (teacher, journalist, doctor); as well as social roles (friend, neighbor, citizen).

We think that we *are* those identities, that they comprise the self. Not so, say most spiritual teachers, theologians, and mystics. But who are we when unmoored from those identities? Who are we when the self's familiar shores recede?

≈

I first came upon the concept of unselfing while reading about two twentieth-century philosophers. One, Iris Murdoch, is most widely known as a novelist, but she also was a respected philosophy tutor at Oxford. The other, Simone Weil, was a French social philosopher and activist who has been described as a mystic. Both had studied Buddhism. Both argued that an attentive way of being is necessary if we are to better behold others and the world around us. And both noted how our egotistic self-preoccupation intrudes upon that attentiveness.

Murdoch contends that the anxious ego blocks us from truly seeing others. In *The Sovereignty of the Good,* she describes the process of *unselfing* as a stilling of our "fat relentless ego" so that we may attend to the world outside the self. Witnessing beauty can be an "occasion for 'unselfing.'" Murdoch describes suddenly seeing a hovering kestrel while she was in an anxious state of mind: "In a moment everything is altered. The brooding self . . . has disappeared. There is nothing now but kestrel."

Weil described a method for unselfing that she called "decreation." The essayist Anne Carson explains that by the process of decreation, Weil wanted to dislodge her ego-self "from a centre where she cannot stay because staying there blocks God." Weil's *decreation* doesn't refer to the destruction of the ego, as the word seems to suggest. Rather, the ego steps aside. When we are not *self*-centered, we can become *God*-centered, according to Weil.

Unselfing could be viewed as the eclipsing of the ego. When the moon eclipses the sun, the solar corona—usually hidden by the sun's blaze—grows visible. Eclipses are periodic and brief. Likewise, the ego's strident light is eclipsed during moments of unselfing—and an inner light is fleetingly revealed.

Photo by Adam McCoid

IN THE EVENING, WE'LL DANCE

≈

The process of becoming self-less resembles a wave that dissolves back into the ocean or a river that empties into the sea. Throughout the ages and in most cultures, people have devised practices to attain this state. By their prayerful, whirling dance, Sufi dervishes seek to enter an ecstatic trance, abandon the self, and attain unity with God. Practices such as meditative retreats or the recitation of a mantra may have similar aims.

Initiation rituals can provide another avenue to self-abandonment. The initiate symbolically dies, relinquishing past self-constructs as the ego's grip loosens. Some Indigenous peoples practice vision quests, during which the initiate symbolically dies to the child-self and transitions into adulthood. During their consecration rites, medieval Christian anchorites underwent a ceremony that resembled a funeral. Following their initiation, the anchorites withdrew to cells adjacent to churches. Henceforth, they were considered dead to the world and reborn to a spiritual life.

Unselfing doesn't occur solely in religious or spiritual contexts. As I accompanied Dick through his dementia, I learned to set aside the self and its need for control in order to be present to him. My ego-self had to step back so that I could be open to what might arise.

When we concentrate deeply upon a task, "the self disappears. We seem to fall utterly into the object of our attention, or else vanish into attentiveness itself," observes Jane Hirshfield, a poet. Hirshfield says we "fall," we "vanish," when immersed in an undertaking. An old, rarely used word, *immerge*, captures her ideas well. *Immerge* conveys the idea of merging: *im* (in) + *merge* (to fuse, to unite). In the eighteenth century, *immerge* was used to describe the process of disappearing into something else, resulting in the loss of identity.

Others describe this state of absorption as being captivated, enthralled, or spellbound, as if a magic charm has been cast. It might happen while writing a poem, listening to music, weeding in the garden, practicing free throws, or noticing the wind as it ruffles a lake. We enter the flow, swept up by a powerful current of deep concentration. We're carried away. We lose ourselves.

≈

Some refer to the ego as "imperial." It doesn't want to abandon its throne. "This crown is heavy," said Dick after he'd had yet another small stroke in the year before his death. I believe that "this crown" might have been a metaphor for his egoic self.

During the later stages of dementia, persons may lose their ego-selves. As a result, the geriatrician Sam Fazio observes that they "can connect on both a deeper and simpler level—heart to heart or soul to soul rather than mind to mind."

When he reached the late stages of dementia, the burden of Dick's imperial crown lightened. He moved inward, and our mind-to-mind dialogue fell silent. At times, we'd commune heart to heart or soul to soul. I sought to accompany him on this inward passage, but I'd often stumble.

I wanted to elucidate the mystery of my husband's unselfing, so I sought out the works of others. Many Eastern and Western spiritual teachers, poets, philosophers, and mystics address the need to unself in order to realize one's deeper being. I jotted down a profusion of passages from my readings, such as *"To be hollow is to be filled"* (Lao Tzu, Taoist philosopher) and *"Everything that is to receive must and ought to be empty"* (Meister Eckhart, Christian mystic).

I rummaged through my library, pulling books off the shelves. They piled up on the worn oak table: volumes of poetry; a compilation of sayings by Jesus, Buddha, Krishna, and Lao Tzu; titles such as *The Enlightened Heart*, *The Inner Journey*, and *The Perennial Philosophy*.

≈

Dick may have provided me with an answer. I found it in his copy of Aldous Huxley's *The Perennial Philosophy*. He'd carefully transcribed a passage of Huxley's in the margins of that tattered blue volume:

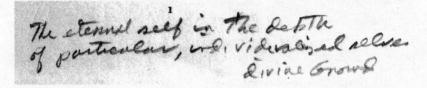

Huxley's words suggested a definition of the unselfed self. It is "the eternal self in the depth of particular, individualized selves . . . akin to the divine Ground." It is revealed when we detach from our particular, individual ego-selves and unself.

The *eternal self, divine ground, true thing, ground of being, inner self, deeper self, Atman, Tao,* or *essence*: We use such words to describe our innermost being. But these terms are only signposts that point toward the ineffable. Along with the poet Fanny Howe, I wondered, "Can something unknown be in-known?"

One reaches the limits of language. And yet I have this stack of books in front of me. Inside, thousands of words swarm across white pages—all of which seek to elucidate the inner self. On a page in *The Divine Within*, Aldous Huxley uses the metaphor of walking on a tightrope to describe the route from the known to the in-known. On one end of the rope, we gather our perceptions and analyze them via language. On the other end, we "drop the language and go on into the experience."

In order to tell you about the unselfed self that I witnessed in my husband, I must walk that wire. I confess my sense of inadequacy as I twist together strands of observations to form the tightrope. How can I describe the ineffable? I'm hunting for something that's beyond my normal experience and beyond my usual lexicon.

I can't "drop the language," yet I want to describe the invisible center that was revealed in my husband at times.

≈

While in that inner world, Dick was silent. He'd sit motionless for hours, watching the sky or the wind on the water. Dementia's turmoil stilled as he gazed at Lake Superior's roiling waves on an autumn afternoon. He watched as dusk descended over little Doan Lake, watched as darkness deepened. He sat, utterly still, before waters both placid and rough, present to the experience. He'd rest his hands in his lap. He didn't speak; he, who loved language.

He moved into and out of that inner place during his final few years. He straddled two worlds, as described by the Sufi poet Rumi:

"I sit on the threshold. / On the threshold are they alone / whose language is silence."

≈

When I recall Dick's last years, two words recur: *presence* and *luminousness*. Dick had an aura about him whenever he spoke in his language of silence. Those moments resembled T. S. Eliot's "still point in the turning world." The wheeling world stills at the resounding sound of a rung bell or the pooling of light around a candle. When Dick entered that stillness, he became a presence.

The philosopher Amelie Rorty delineates the many ways humans have defined persons throughout history, such as characters, individuals, and presences. She describes presences as beings-beyond-ego who exude "immense gravity and density." One can't willfully determine to become a presence. Rorty reminds us that, like a state of grace, presence goes "beyond achievement and willfulness." It's a "return of the unchartable soul."

Presences create a mood to which others respond; they can transform us just by their being. When I'd find Dick in that placid state, I'd sit next to him, match my breath to his, and absorb his calm. My busyness gave way to presence. Everything else fell away.

Others had this experience with my husband, too. One friend recalls that "being with Dick called me into the present moment. And maybe that was what made it profound." Another friend, Sylvia, observed that Dick "had that luminosity." He was, she said, "only presence. He was just being there with no frills, yet very aware." No frills: Dick lived in the now, lacking the memories and plans that tow us back to the past or toward the future. He was wholly present in the moment, which is a state many seek.

People who have dementia lack the "ability to reason, or to cover up" who they really are, observes the gerontologist Tena Alonzo. Therefore, "you see the loveliness of the soul—it is bare for everyone to acknowledge."

≈

Those moments of presence transfigured Dick. He seemed beatific. His eyes were luminous. Even with his eyes closed, his face shone. As I write this, I glance up at a photo of him, the one that appears at the beginning of this essay. A framed black-and-white print hangs to the left of my desk. Dick looks lit from within. Like a moon, his countenance shines down on me.

I'm not attempting to mythologize Dick; this essay isn't hagiographic. I'm reporting what I—and others—witnessed in him. Those who work in dementia care have observed similar transformations. As the disease progresses, persons with dementia "journey deeper into the centre of our being, into our Spirit," according to Christine Bryden, who wrote about her early-onset dementia.

When I'd encounter Dick in this state, it caused me to wonder, "What is it that I'm feeling right now?" One day, the answer came: "I'm in the presence of something holy."

Holy is a word I don't use. I refer to *beauty, wonder, mystery,* or *awe* when I speak of the sublime in the arts and in the natural world. But holy? And yet, there it was, my inner voice strong and clear: This is holy.

It seemed too mystical. Too woo-woo. So I didn't tell anyone. I explained it away. I suspected that the word *holy* came to mind because I was in love with the man. But the adjectives I'd use to describe Dick were never in the elevated realm of *holy*. I thought of him as honest, earthy, eager, funny, fidgety, sexy, stubborn, kind, gentle, and bright. Even wise. But never *holy*.

It was the experience, not the man, that was holy.

≈

Aging can be another form of unselfing. I recently witnessed age's many diminishments in my mother, with the decline of her vision, hearing, and vigor. She shrank, becoming shorter and thinner. She seemed to quietly recede.

As people age and face death, they may begin to lose the separate self. They may accept that loss with equanimity, as my mother did, or feel terror at the thought of it. In the late stages, dementia often is accompanied by a similar loss of the self. I witnessed this passage in my husband.

≈

And then he died. In bereavement "we start to see how conditional who-I-am-ness really is," observes Pema Khandro Rinpoche, a Buddhist Lama.

Who was I? I knew who I no longer was: a spouse, companion, caregiver, lover, the beloved. Grief enshrouds the bereaved. My mind often seemed absent, my body numb. Grief scoured me out.

In some cultures, roadside shrines serve to shepherd the spirits of the deceased to another realm. The grieving continue to travel in this earthly realm, but the signposts are gone. I could have used some shepherding, like the deceased.

≈

During my struggle to write about Dick's unselfing, more and more books cluttered the large oak table. I wanted an authority to enlighten me; I was inadequate to the task. Or so I thought.

Then I turned to my old journals, where I found pages filled with ruminations on humility. Dick and I discussed humility more than once, because I couldn't comprehend it. I was a young woman; the ego

IN THE EVENING, WE'LL DANCE

I'd cobbled together had been hard-won. Dick cheerfully informed me that humility "is one of life's most important lessons." He accepted his limitations and embraced the fact that he was "only human."

Among my musings, I discovered this entry from 1991: *Dick says the best thing one can learn is humility. But what is it to be humble?* I answered my own question: *It's to bow your head down, to relinquish the ego self. It is to be nameless, in a sense. And that's the terror of it. What's left when 'self' is abandoned?* Again, I answered the question: *Spirit or soul, of course. It's joyous and liberating, too, if one can get past the fear.*

I'd grappled with how to write about the inexpressible, about what remains when the egoic self is jettisoned. I'd read the words of mystics, poets, and philosophers. Then I discovered my own words, in a journal entry written more than three decades ago.

I didn't remember what I had articulated then. The fleeting awareness I had come to resembled the ripples that radiate around a stone thrown into a lake. The ripples faded away, water closed over the stone, and it sank to the bottom. The knowledge resided in me, at a subconscious level. I needed to circle back, dive down, and recollect (re-collect) it. I knew, but I didn't know that I knew.

CHAPTER 22

Pursue Spiritual Growth

The moments of Dick's unselfing that I—and others—witnessed weren't miraculous. They had a history. Aspects of my life, of his life, and of our lives together had prepared us.

When I was a teen, I'd often roam my small hometown alone. One autumn, I walked to the town's edge at sunset. I stood facing a hayfield and, beyond it, a fringe of trees. I watched the sun slowly meld into the horizon.

As I watched, I saw that the light shone *through* the trees. The light stood behind and shone through everything. I thought, "That light is god." It was an epiphany, a sort of panentheistic (all-in-god) awareness. The light pervaded all created things.

It reminded me of the benediction I've loved since childhood. The minister stood in front of the congregation, formed the sign of the cross, and asked the Lord to make His face shine on us and give us peace. I'd basked in those words, intoned at the conclusion of Sunday services. That face had shone upon me; it gave me peace. It also gave me joy.

Ever since, I've been drawn to paintings of trees in the fading light. A print of Gustav Klimt's "Beech Forest" hangs above my bed, the ground littered with leaves of rust and gold, shafts of late light illuminating lithe grey trees. George Inness's ethereal "The Home of the Heron" is displayed above my piano. The sun has set; the world glows, imbuing the grass, the water, and the trees with a dusky gold.

Inness wanted his landscapes to express the "reality of the unseen." I know what Inness meant. At the edge of the hayfield, I saw what I saw with my eyes: the field, a line of trees, a setting sun. That was the material reality. The light shining *through* everything was the reality of the unseen. I apprehended it with my whole being.

Years later, that insight at the field's edge enabled me to balance dualities: the material world and the world of the spirit, the seen and the unseen. And it informed my understanding of my husband's dementia: his presence and absence, his self and not-self.

≈

The self he was when healthy led to Dick's moments of unselfing. From the time I met him, he had an interest in spirituality. The poet Mary Oliver writes, "What I mean by spirituality is not theology, but attitude." Our spirituality was short on theology, but Dick and I shared an attitude of awe. We believed that the sacred manifests itself in the world. We saw the world as "charged with the grandeur of God," the line from the poet Gerard Manley Hopkins that often hums in my head.

In one of Dick's notebooks from the 1980s, he'd written, *The Spiritual Way? I would say it is the seeking after and developing of that which is our true (good) nature.* His resolutions at the onset of 1985 included this entry: *Seek spiritual growth (read philosophy and religion; pursue questions/confront conscience).*

On January 1, 1998—the year his memory loss became apparent—he resolved to *pursue spiritual growth via reading, meditation, and shedding anger—on a daily basis. Cultivate understanding and compassion.*

In 2001, he clipped a cartoon from *The New Yorker* and tucked it into his agenda book. The cartoonist Pat Byrnes depicted two monks in the meditation pose. One turns to the other and asks, "Are you not thinking what I'm not thinking?"

Recently, I opened Dick's copy of *The Choice Is Always Ours*, an anthology of writings on the spiritual way. A yellowed sheet of notebook paper fell into my lap. On it, Dick had written: *There is inherent in you the desire to find your true self, a craving for knowledge of the right direction/orientation, giving a sense of meaning, purpose, reality, eternity.*

IN THE EVENING, WE'LL DANCE

≈

Dick and I usually did not say grace. Rather than praying, we practiced a moment of silence before our evening meals. We'd give thanks, each in his or her own way. I'd begin by silently expressing gratitude for the husband at my side and the dog at my feet. The rest of my grace varied; I might give thanks for the food we'd prepared, for our friends, or for a splendid sunset. We respected one another's silence, so I never knew what Dick chose to silently convey.

Years into his dementia, Dick suddenly decided that he wanted our dinners to begin with a spoken prayer. Perhaps the ritual of prayer was flotsam he clung to as dementia engulfed him. His choice of a grace evolved gradually. He tried out variations, such as, "May the good Lord look upon us with peace and tranquility," and "We thank you for this day, oh Lord. May we have good will toward all men and women." Yet another variant—my favorite—was, "May we have peace like a bell."

Finally, he settled on a version, which he seldom failed to recite. He'd reach across the table to hold my hand, his signal that it was time to say grace. Then he'd bow his head and say, "May the good Lord bless us and keep us forever more. Amen."

But that prayer wasn't his only expression of gratitude. He would declare, "Life is beautiful," especially during our daily walks.

One summer day in 2011 we strolled from our home to a small park on Crystal Lake. "Our lake," Dick called it. As we walked, he asked me once again for the name of the couple who live in the yellow house next to ours. "Who lives across the way?"

"The Godfreys," I replied.

"The Dodfreys," he said.

"No. Godfrey. As in the words *god* and *free*."

Dick was silent for a while. He gazed at the lake, the trees, and the sky. Then he said, "Free God from his perch."

Dick's striking remark—from where did it arise? Due to the dementia, most of his past was gone and he couldn't envision the future. Instead, he lived moment to moment. As Archibald MacLeish writes, "There is no dusk to be, / There is no dawn that was, / Only there's now, and now, / And the wind in the grass."

According to the Bible, the world itself—the lakes, the trees, the wind in the grass—is the very "body of God." Perhaps that's what my husband was saying, in his own way. *Free God from his perch*: Liberate God from the image of a remote, on-high-in-the-sky being. As Dick looked at the world around him, his mind uncluttered by future or past, he saw the body of God everywhere.

≈

A year later, Dick and I rested on a bench next to the lake. We sat quietly, facing the water.

Then Dick spoke: "I want to say something." He turned to me and touched me with his fingertips: my right thigh, my breastbone, the top of my head, my lips.

"You're beautiful," he said, finally.

Another benediction.

PART 5

Leave-taking

CHAPTER 23

You Are Me

The swamp-margin lies at the edge of the cemetery in George Saunders' *Lincoln in the Bardo*. It's the furthest margin in a marginal place called the bardo, where spirits linger between death and rebirth. The face of one denizen, Mr. Papers, has faded into an unrecognizable smudge. Mr. Papers calls out to passersby, "Cannery anyhelpmate? Come. To. Heap me? Cannery help? . . Place hepMay."

I've heard such calls: my mother's nursing home roommate, quietly pleading, "Help meee, help meee, help meee," as she sank into forgetfulness. A man's cries careening down the halls of the geriatric psychiatric ward, "Helpme!Helpme!Helpme!" They ripped through the quiet of my husband's room, unsettling us.

I felt like I was crossing into the swamp-margin when I visited my husband in a memory care facility. I'd entered an "anteroom to another realm," as the author Rebecca Mead puts it. The residents often were inarticulate and adrift, like Mr. Papers. They were not fully there, but not yet elsewhere. They lingered in the anteroom.

≈

Waiting rooms are the anterooms with which we are most familiar. Recall the hours spent in hospital waiting rooms, slumped in chairs. Time's pace slackens, the room grows close with thick air, sultry, like a claggy day in England. Another type of anteroom is the narthex, a space near the entrance of early churches. The narthex separated penitents from the congregation.

Such a space also might be described as *threshold* or *liminal*. Liminal places are transitional and therefore ambiguous. We can lose our bearings and grow disoriented in these unmapped no-man's lands. Historically, a "no-man's land" divided countries before there were borders. To be in a no-man's land was to be neither in Spain nor in France. Neither here nor there.

Nursing homes and memory care units are neither here nor there: they're in a community, yet marginal to it. The residents often are socially isolated, compatriots in an involuntary outsiderhood.

Dick and I understood outsiderhood. When we built our log cabin, we chose to live outside of the mainstream. For almost thirty years, we hauled water and heated with a small wood stove. We worked within the community while remaining at the social margins. When his dementia became more noticeable, we continued to be both *a part of* and *apart from*.

≈

The night of Dick's death, we were apart from ordinary life, and we had slipped outside of time.

Our many years together had come down to a small room and a narrow bed, which I shared with him. The memory persists: That night his room was isolated and drifting.

The windows of Dick's room at Oak Hill looked out on October's browned grass and barren trees, while a door opened onto a large space: kitchen, dining area, lounge. But that night, the windows and his bed all shifted places. And the door did not open onto anything.

In the room of my memory, the walls are bare. The photos of his children, grandchildren, and us; his photos of Spain; his daughter's drawings; the folkloric painting of a village; the Irish calendar above his bed—all are absent.

We floated alone together in the bed, contained within a vast space. The other rooms, the other residents, fell away. What remained was my husband and me and the bed and the room. How could this be?

It wasn't a dream. I didn't sleep at all; I talked and sang to him throughout that night. Like me, the artist Marion Coutts was alone with her husband as he died of cancer. She writes, "We have stopped being anywhere at all. We are way outside, out of culture, place, gender. I do not know where we are but I feel very sure of myself here."

I was sure that he'd die that night; I was resigned to that death. My mind spun his bed around so it faced west instead of its true eastward position. East: where the sun, symbol of life, rises. West: the direction of a dying sun, of darkness.

≈

In the book of Genesis, God divides the light from the darkness, the day from the night. The first chapter of Genesis contains a counting of days. Over those six days, many things come into being: the heavens and seas; the earth, its grasses and trees; the sun and moon; fish and fowl. Creatures of every kind. Man. Woman. Genesis—the story and the word—represents beginnings: of time, of creation.

Exodus follows Genesis. Exodus means *departure*, from the Greek *ex*, or *out*, and *hodos*, a way, a journey. *Exhodos*. A journey out. Sometimes the exodus means fleeing, as it was for the Israelites. Sometimes it is a solemn procession. And sometimes it is the literal journey out, death. Birth, a genesis. Death, an exodus.

Genesis. Exodus. The rhyming sound of the two words charmed me as a child charged with memorizing the order of the biblical books. The charm continued with Leviticus. Gen-e-sis. Ex-o-dus. Le-vit-i-cus. The little rhyme ends abruptly with Numbers, followed by the roiling thunder of Deuteronomy.

Say the words: Genesis-Exodus-Genesis-Exodus. They swing like a pendulum, a metronome marking off time. Tick-tock. The beginning: Let there be light. Tick-tock. The end: And then there was night.

≈

My friend Yvonne had tucked into a small room at the local hospital to view videos on birthing. When she finished her work and headed for the parking lot, she passed through the lounge of the adjacent nursing home. She saw two residents slumped over in their chairs. But instead of cringing inwardly at their frail, piteous state, she stopped dead in her tracks.

It seemed to Yvonne that the two elders were in an anteroom to another realm. They were lingering in the margins between life and death.

Yvonne felt as if she'd witnessed something holy. She told me, "They looked as though they were filled with light. They were so beautiful I wanted to go over and touch them, to be near that beautiful light. Then I realized that they were in the birth canal, just like the babies I had just watched being delivered. They would soon be born into a new realm—a realm of light."

A *regressus ad uterum* (return to the womb) is included in some initiation rituals. It requires an initiate to descend into the darkness before a symbolic rebirth. And in some cultures, a dying person is put into a fetal position, to symbolize rebirth.

≈

The scholar Gisela Webb, whose mother had Alzheimer's, describes dementia as "the great unlearning." She wonders if what we witness in dementia might be "a kind of return to our origins—an Edenic pre-self-conscious, pre-dualistic state."

Note that Webb uses the word *return*, not *regression*. To *regress* is to move backward, usually to a worse, less developed state. Dick was a mature person when I met him, and he remained so until the end. He could be playful, but never childish. A person with dementia "will never view the world around him the same way a small child would," asserts G. Allen Power, a geriatrician. To treat someone with dementia like a small child would negate the many life experiences he or she has had.

The process Webb describes might be thought of as a retracing. *To re-trace* is to make one's way back, to return to the source. As the disease progressed, Dick would speak as if Doris, his aunt, were alive. She had died in 2006. Then he was with his mother, dead in 1961, and his father, who died when Dick was six. Later, he travelled back another generation: "I'm wondering if I should call Grandpa Jim. And Grandma," he said the year before his death.

I think that Dick may have revisited his own child-self, as well—the young boy who still had his parents, Aunt Doris, and grandparents in

IN THE EVENING, WE'LL DANCE

his world. A few months before his death, an aide heard him talking to someone late a night. She peeked into his room. There was no one there.

"Come here," he said, patting his bed. "Sit by me." He talked as if he were speaking to a little child. Then he said, "Run along now" and fell into silence and sleep.

≈

I was struck by a photograph by Lennart Nilsson that a friend posted on Facebook. It was of a sixteen-week-old fetus, exploring its body with its hands. That remarkable photo is one of a sequence that depicts the developing fetus as it floats in the womb's salty waters.

The photo reminded me of the last months of Dick's life, when he was often bedridden. He'd lift a leg, then slowly run his hands along his own thigh and lower leg, exploring his extremities. He was tracing the territory of his body.

He would also hold up his hand—sometimes left, sometimes right—and form a circle with the tips of his thumb and index finger. He held his fingers in a graceful arc, his hand fixed in this position for several minutes. It reminded me of a *mudra,* which is Sanskrit for *gesture.* His gesture was similar to a mudra that helps one feel calm and present.

One day, Dick made a circle with his thumb and index finger, then held it up to his right eye, forming a sort of telescope that focuses one's vision. *Telescope,* from the Greek, means "far-seeing." Dick kept this position for almost a half-hour. The next day, he had another stroke.

≈

In Nilsson's photos, the embryonic face is a series of cavities at five weeks. By the eighth week, two black ovals gleam beneath the high white dome of the head.

Nilsson's photo of an eight-week-old embryo is hauntingly similar to a self-portrait by William Utermohlen, an American figurative painter who developed Alzheimer's in his sixties. He produced self-portraits as the disease progressed, adjusting his technique as his motor skills and spatial awareness declined.

In 2000, a year before he could no longer draw, Utermohlen used a pencil to create a spare, abstract depiction of himself, "Head." Under a large skull and bulging forehead, he loosely sketched in a nose and mouth. The eyes are dark and firm: two round, black blots. "This head seems fetal, with its helmet-like cranium and open, black eyes," observes Patrice Polini, a psychoanalyst. Most of the face is a smudge, resembling the visage of Mr. Papers of the swamp-margin.

Soon after his diagnosis, Utermohlen said that he wanted to convey what was happening to him via his art. His paintings continued to communicate his thoughts after he lost his verbal abilities. Utermohlen's drawing of the fetal-like head was a self-portrait. What did he communicate about himself with this work, which he completed near the end of his life? Perhaps the artist had envisioned the retracing of his self back to its origins, when he was at the threshold before birth.

Utermohlen's colorful watercolors, referred to as "Masks," contrast with the stark penciled portraits. The face shapes blur into the paper, the mouth either absent or a smudge. Intense blue eyes peer out at the viewer. Like all of Utermohlen's late works, the watercolors seek to depict dementia from the inside. They lay bare his awareness of his own dissolution, even as he continued to create.

≈

Dick's legs buckled as I helped him to the car on the day I moved him to Oak Hill, a facility close to our home. It was March 28, 2014. He'd had another small stroke, called a TIA (transient ischemic attack).

The TIA that morning left Dick unable to walk. Unsteady on his feet, he grew uncertain as to how to stand, walk, or sit down in a chair. His long limbs seemed disconnected from his torso, alien objects he attempted to maneuver in space. His motor cortex struggled to control the complex sequence of turns, bends, and folds our bodies make with unconscious ease. It took three of us to maneuver him into a wheelchair. When he was finally seated, he listed markedly to one side. He attempted to speak but was incoherent. As we waited at the clinic to see his physician, Dick eyes were unfocused and his mouth agape.

IN THE EVENING, WE'LL DANCE

≈

I sang to him while we idled in the dreary patient room. I hoped that he would sing along; the words of familiar songs might help him to regain speech. People who have difficulties with speech often can still sing, since musical memory is located in different areas of the brain than language.

It was hard for the both of us—for me to witness him in such a state and for him to be in such a state. He was fearful, as was I. To reassure him, I smiled and held him in a loving gaze.

Suddenly, he focused his eyes, looked directly at me, and said, "You are me, and me is you."

The statement struck me. So did its ungrammatical nature. That was atypical. Even when he was in the last stages of dementia, Dick would correct an aide's grammar. If she said, "My husband don't like cities," Dick would interject: "Doesn't!"

Was the incorrect grammar a result of the TIA? Normally, even with the dementia, he would have said, "You are me, and I am you."

On further thought, I realized that, unlike the correct construction, the two sides of his statement mirrored one another: *You are Me / Me is You.*

Perhaps that was it. However it came to be, that mirrored structure gave his declaration a poetic beauty—a beauty that suited the insight.

≈

"Even though you tie a hundred knots, the string remains one."
—Rumi

I've arrived at another margin. I hesitate, teetering at the edge of knowing. When Dick said, "You are me," it could simply have been a recognition of our symbiosis—a closeness that grew out of our four decades together. On the other hand, when he made that striking statement he was emerging from a liminal place between worlds: from the realm of a stroke that temporarily robbed him of speech and mobility, back to the daily world, with his wife in a chair facing him, singing to him. I wondered if his statement referred to our symbiosis or if it was an epiphany.

Then I read Jill Bolte Taylor's account of her massive stroke in *My Stroke of Insight*. Following her stroke, Taylor found herself unable to walk or speak intelligibly, like Dick after his TIA. Her brain's language centers "grew increasingly silent." Taylor often slipped into a sense of serenity and peace, despite her awareness that she urgently needed help or she might die. She describes those moments of calm as being in "the wisdom of my dementia."

Taylor explains that the brain's two hemispheres "work intimately with one another" but process information differently. The stroke occurred in her brain's left hemisphere, which is dominant in her work as a neuroscientist. It's linear and sequential. It analyzes, recognizes patterns, categorizes, and "thrives on details." It's our language center, busily naming, defining, categorizing.

Taylor became acutely aware of her right brain as her left hemisphere hemorrhaged and began to shut down. The right hemisphere synthesizes, thinks in pictures, remains in the present moment, and is intuitive, spontaneous, and imaginative.

As the right hemisphere became dominant, Taylor began to lose her sense of solidity and boundaries. She felt fluid. It reminded me of Mr. Papers and Utermohlen's watercolors, the faces dissolving. Separations melted away and "the energy of everything blended together." In this state, she lost her sense of individuality and became aware of "'being at *one*' with the universe." That realization of oneness was her stroke of insight.

≈

When Taylor's stroke shut down her left brain, she experienced oneness. I believe that Dick's TIA had the same effect.

People throughout history have reported experiences of oneness or nonduality. Duality sets up two contrasting or opposing concepts, such as spirit and matter, mind and body, light and dark. The theologian Cynthia Bourgeault points out that "a system based in duality can't possibly perceive oneness." To perceive oneness is to experience the unity that underlies existence. The separation between self and other falls away; the "me" dissolves. "I" am the wave that crests, then falls and merges with the vast sea.

To experience oneness, a person must forget or transcend the everyday world. The medical ethicist Stephen G. Post speculates that people with dementia who appear to be oblivious might actually be in "that world of betwixt and between," that liminal, transitional place outside of ordinary time.

Perhaps those seemingly absent persons in the dementia ward are "on a spiritual plane of consciousness," posits Post. He notes that in several Buddhist and Hindu cultures, "the deeply forgetful are thought of as on the path of detachment and Enlightenment."

It turns out that Dick had been seeking that path years before his dementia. When I opened our copy of *The Enlightened Heart*, I found that he'd marked this line in a poem: "Be at peace in the oneness of things."

"How are you today?" I asked Dick two months before his death.

"Perfect," he replied.

CHAPTER 24

In the Evening, We'll Dance

A week before he died, my husband said, "I hurt." Such a report was rare; it alarmed me. I asked him where he hurt. He couldn't say.

"Here?" I asked, as I tapped his abdomen with my fingertips. No response. I moved up to his chest, neck, forehead. "Here? Here? Here?" Nothing.

It's difficult to know whether a person with dementia is ill or dying. They often can't tell you how they feel or where they hurt. "He doesn't understand what's happening to him," some said as he neared the end of his life.

My husband had been failing for two years. One month before his death in October of 2015, he was admitted to hospice for the third and final time. He knew that he was dying. He had been preparing himself, preparing me.

In the year before he died: "He can't self-report," I'd say, my four-word compression of the story: his memory gone; most of his mobility, gone; much of his cognitive ability and language, gone. But, at some level, he still *understood.*

Ten months before he died: "End. Are we going to the cemetery?" my husband asked.

Nine months before:

"Where are you going?" I asked,
as he strained to get up from his
wheelchair.
"To see the wizard," he replied.
"Why do you want to see the wizard?"
I asked.
"To ask him a few questions."

Eight months:

"Almost free," he whispered after a
small stroke, as he struggled to hold
his body upright in a chair.

Five months:

"Have you seen the dying man?" he
asked me. "He's ahead, on the road."

Four months:

"I'm still here," he said. Then,
"Something's wrong with me."

Three months:

*The authors of textbooks on death
tell us that it's wise to pay attention
to what the dying say. They may
use symbolic language to allude
to their impending death, such as
talking about preparations for a
trip.*
"Is it like a journey?" he asked me.

Two months:

"Time to go," he declared.
"Where?" I asked.
"Far away."

IN THE EVENING, WE'LL DANCE

One month:

Experts explain that dying persons sometimes will say a deceased loved one—a "spirit visitor"—is coming for them. This is called a visitation. Research suggests that such end-of-life visions "hold profound meaning for dying people." They help them to accept their death as it draws near.

"Doris is looking for me," he said. His aunt Doris had been dead for many years.
"Do you think she'll find you?" I asked.
"Yes, she will," he said with certainty. "She's over there." He pointed to a corner of his room.
"Where?"
"Across the river."

Three weeks before he died:

"My husband is dying." I practiced saying this without crying.

In the end:

An authority on the psychology of aging suggests that people who have dementia "may not be able to understand that they are dying." But in the days prior to his death, Dick said:

"I have to get through this."
"I want to go home now."
"Is it about time to cross over?"
"I've had enough of life."
"Death."

ANNE-MARIE ERICKSON

≈

One day in July of 2015, an elderly woman was dying. Her room at Oak Hill Assisted Living was next to Dick's. An aide observed that he was very subdued that afternoon. He sat in front of his mirror for two hours, gazing at his reflection. The aide asked him what he was looking at. "An old man," he replied.

Later that afternoon Dick wheeled himself away from the mirror to the windows in his room. He stared at the green world outside. Perhaps it was his way of fleeing Death as it crept into the rooms around him.

≈

In early September, I dreamed that my husband had died. A man with a stethoscope said, "His heart stopped." Then he turned away from me and walked down a long hallway. I went into a room with a single bed, stripped bare. I knew then that Dick had died. I kept repeating, "I want him to be *here!*"

The following morning, I cried, then got up and cooked a pot of garden tomatoes, reserving a few for him. Cooking was a way to deal with my grief. I imagined that the food would sustain him. It didn't. Some days he didn't eat at all. When he did, the food furnished little nourishment to his aging body as it grew less able to absorb nutrients. A slender man already, he grew rawboned. Skeletal.

≈

Some people speculated that Dick's love for me was keeping him alive. They'd suggest that I give him permission to leave me, to reassure him that I'd be all right. I'd done so several times, including once in September. Most likely I'd used a euphemism, such as "let go" or "rest." Then we sat together quietly for a while.

Suddenly, he said, "She'll be okay."

I knew that he had understood my reassurance. I would let him go.

I also knew that it wasn't only his love for me that kept Dick alive. I'd explain to others, "Yes, he loves me. But he loves life, too." As he'd often told me, "Life is beautiful."

IN THE EVENING, WE'LL DANCE

≈

On September 24, 2015, the thirty-seventh day before he died, my husband lay supine in his bed, feverish and unresponsive. The hospice doctor and nurse huddled with me in a far corner of his room, voices lowered as they murmured "any time"—perhaps three hours, three days, three weeks.

"He's such a beautiful man. I love him so much," I replied. Then I wept.

Now I wonder if he heard me declaring my love and crying in the corner of his room, because the next day he rose from his bed. The aides gathered him up into his wheelchair and rolled him out to the dining room. I sat by his side as he ate, talked, and laughed. Coming upon this sight, the visiting hospice nurse opened her eyes wide in surprise.

This was not the first time he seemed to be nearing death. This was not the first time he had rebounded—as if he were a tennis ball smacked into a wall, then springing back.

≈

The first time he bounced back and was discharged from hospice, I wailed in the margins of my 2014 planner, "I'm upset. Depressed. How long will this go on? I fear the vegetative state." I read this now and it sounds both heartless and heartfelt, filled both with self-pity and with compassion for my husband.

The vegetative state is the final of "four degrees of incoherence." That's how an early researcher labeled the stages of dementia. In the last stage, higher brain functions are gone; instinctive and voluntary actions, gone. The victims become "immobile, their bodies assuming grotesque positions as they stiffen or slump toward death," writes Sherwin Nuland in *How We Die.*

Dick never reached the vegetative state, but often he'd sleep for days and refuse all food. Then aides would worm a syringe into a corner of his mouth and squirt Ensure into him, while I'd wipe the drool from his beard.

≈

At a conference on Alzheimer's, heads nodded in understanding when a speaker addressed the oft-unspoken wish: "I wish it was over." *I* being the caregiver. *It* being the relentless decline of their loved one. *Over* meaning death.

The prognosis for dementia, starkly described by Nuland, is "the inexorable certainty of deterioration and death." *Inexorable*: that which cannot be moved by entreaty, pleas, or prayers.

≈

On September 27, three days after Dick had been admitted to hospice for the last time, our friend Sylvia sat quietly by his side, her back straight, eyes alert. He rested. She observed him.

"He's busy working through unfinished things," she told me. "He's at a threshold."

The word *threshold* refers to a point at which something begins or changes. A decision or choice is made. Then one steps over, entering a new stage in life. It could be during a rite of passage, such as a marriage or the death of a loved one. Or when we face our own death. At such moments, we may be jolted out of old ways of seeing and old ways of being—if we are willing to cross over the threshold.

"To cross over" is a euphemism for "to die." Some stumble or stomp over that threshold to their deaths. Some tread lightly. Others cling desperately to the door jambs. My husband paused.

≈

On the last day of September, just one week after the hospice doctor had whispered "any time," I wheeled my husband onto a bus for the annual Oak Hill autumn leaf tour. As the bus wended its way on rural roads, I'd exclaim, "Look!"—at the lakes, leaves, and fading fields.

Dick ignored me. Whatever he saw dancing in front of his eyes was far more enticing. Perhaps butterflies, I thought, or silky filaments bearing seeds. As he hallucinated, he'd reach out, pluck those minute mysteries from the air, and place them on his lap, in his cupped hand, or in the hand of the lady next to him. She thanked him.

Later that afternoon, the last photo was taken of my husband and me together: my head leaning against his forehead, my arms around him, my eyes and smile bright with joy. His face is pallid, his mustache and beard ragged. His eyes are watery, downcast, almost closed. He looks content, yet withdrawn, as if he were partially there, partially elsewhere.

≈

In that last photo of my husband, he's there, yet gone, wavering at a threshold: "Like a shipwreck we die going into ourselves, / . . . / as though we lived falling out of the skin into the soul," wrote Pablo Neruda in his poem "Nothing but Death." Dick had been falling out of his skin and moving into his soul for years.

≈

Our thirty-fourth wedding anniversary was on October 10. I brought him twelve red roses, because he favored red. I found him flushed and feverish, his pulse and breath rapid. I called his children, my sister, and friends. "He's taken a turn for the worse," I said.

That night I stayed on the floor near his bed so I could watch the slight rise and fall of his chest. I lay awake, listening to his breathing, listening for his last words.

People listen for the dying person's last words. They hope to hear a message that will help them make meaning of life, of death. And as their own death nears, some seek to compose such a message. A death poem, called a *jisei*, is an ancient custom in Japan. The poet, often a monk, reflects on his coming demise. But the word "death" usually is not mentioned in a *jisei*. Metaphors—autumn, sunset, withered fields— symbolize life's transience.

Most people don't write death poems. Instead, we have collections of "famous last words." They appear in books, magazines, and online. Oscar Wilde's last words were "This wallpaper and I are fighting a duel to the death. Either it goes or I do." The solemn last words, "Now comes the mystery," were spoken by Henry Ward Beecher, a nineteenth-century clergyman.

≈

Through their last words, people can live on in the memories of others, if those words are repeated in stories or written down. Otherwise, they're ephemeral.

The desire for permanence impels humans to erect monuments, such as statues or gravestones. It's a kind of symbolic immortality. People want to leave a mark on the world that says, "I lived. I accomplished something." Or simply, "I was here," like lovers' initials inscribed inside a heart, carved into a tree.

A person dying of dementia is no longer able to write, "I was here." My husband couldn't. But perhaps he understood at some level that he would live on in his progeny. Two weeks before his death, I asked Dick if he'd like to see his kids. He quickly said, "Yes." Earlier, he'd asked, "Is there a last time for the whole crew to get together?" By the "whole crew," I assumed he meant his children.

Each of his three children came to bid their father farewell during his final days. I believe that he waited for them.

≈

As he grew weaker, so did his voice. Some days, it was reduced to a whisper.

I told him, "You are my love."

He replied slowly, with emphasis, "You - are - my - life."

Ten days before his death, Dick was resting in his bed. I leaned over him and said, "Hello, love."

He opened his eyes and—wordlessly—he stretched his arms out, enfolded me in them, drew me close, and kissed, and kissed, and kissed me.

That night, I returned to his side. He gently stroked my back, held my hands, and kissed me again.

IN THE EVENING, WE'LL DANCE

≈

Five days before his death, I got the call, "Come right away!" The nurse at Oak Hill told me that Dick had collapsed in the bathroom, ashen, shaking, pale legs splotched red, heart pounding. He was breathing rapidly—but still singing "You are my sunshine." Probably to calm himself.

When I arrived, his pulse and breathing remained rapid. The nurse had moved him to his bed, given him morphine, and started him on oxygen, but he continued to gasp for air. It was dire, I knew. I believed that he wouldn't die that day, but I also accepted reality. There comes a point when death is a deliverance. I've seen it in my grandparents, my uncle, my aunt, my father and mother. They declared that they were ready "to go," to die. Death ended their suffering. It was a blessing.

I climbed over Dick into his bed. I pressed my back against the wall, faced him, wrapped my arms around him, and tried to calm him. I stroked his chest, his face. I whispered, "It's okay. It's okay. It's okay." I was reassuring myself as well.

≈

In the biblical telling, God commands man to "cleave unto his wife and they shall be one flesh." *Cleave* means to abide by or with another. Adam is to stick by Eve.

This form of *cleave* derives from the word *clay*, that heavy soil which, when moistened, shaped, and dried, forms ceramics, tile, or brick. Clay is a metaphor for humankind's fleshly form. Man and wife were to be to one flesh, molded together, yet separate.

Cleave also means "to split apart." It's the way we most often use the word. My father wielded a cleaver to butcher a side of beef. Dick and I would cleave chunks of firewood with a splitting maul.

The afternoon of the call, death sought to cleave us asunder. We defied death that day, remaining one flesh, husband and wife cleaving to one another in a narrow bed.

≈

Then he began to sing again, a song unlike any other. It seemed as if he were speaking in tongues, those word-like syllables. Days later, I viewed videos of Pentecostals in the midst of babbling their "divine language." The pitch and volume of their utterances varied, but not the intensity, a rapid ejaculation of harsh noises. This kind of glossolalia was not what I'd heard. My husband sang soft syllables, many "ah," "la," and "ahm" sounds. It most resembled a Sufi chant: the chant echoes the sound of breathing, with a rhythm like a pulse. Sometimes I wish that I'd recorded his song on my phone, but I'd wanted to remain fully present to him.

≈

I stayed with him the rest of that day, only leaving to walk the dog and gather up some bedding and clothes. I moved into his room and slept on a mattress on the floor. I called his kids and sent messages to a few friends.

The next day, his lungs began filling up with fluid. He was so weak that he was unable to respond to the staff or to me.

I'd asked our friend Catherine to get our dog, Phoenix, and bring him to see Dick. When she arrived, I took the dog's leash and walked Phoenix to my husband's bedside. Our ten-year-old dog—without hesitation—leapt up into the hospital bed. He rolled around joyfully, a flurry of ginger-colored fur.

"It's Phoenix, your dog, Phoenix!" I told Dick. He didn't respond to the pandemonium. Nor did he react when I took his hand and brushed it against the dog's silken coat. I was stunned. I'd assumed that Phoenix's visit would rouse Dick.

He loved our dog, who was, as Dick said, "So bright-eyed and full of life." When Dick still lived at home, Phoenix was always by his side. Dick would sing songs to him and tell him, "Phoenix! You're man's best friend." Although Dick occasionally forgot my name, he never forgot Phoenix's.

But even Phoenix's exuberant presence could not elicit a response from Dick.

IN THE EVENING, WE'LL DANCE

≈

During those final days of October, late autumn strode in. It was the time of barren trees and flocking birds. I sat by the window in Dick's room and watched a solitary bird fling itself from a branch and wing against the gusty winds. It glided, then swooped with an updraft until it had flown far away. Grey clouds hovered close, as if clutched to earth's chilled breast. That much I remember.

The rest is fragmentary. Three days before my husband died, a friend came to stay at our home, to take in the mail and feed and walk the dog. Friends took me out to dinner. We gathered around a table in a restaurant, sometimes three, four, five of us. I ate something. Sometimes I had a glass of wine. I joined the conversations. I said things.

"Things!" I'd exclaim to my writing students. "It's such a vague word. Be specific." But vagueness is what those days were about. I moved "in a fog," as they say. Only I didn't see the fog. I didn't even know who the *I* was.

≈

When he still lived at home, one afternoon Dick said to me, "Beautiful evening."

"No, love," I said. "It's not quite evening. Look out the windows. See? The sun's still shining."

"Well, in the evening, we'll dance," he replied.

I made note of our exchange in my commonplace book. It delighted me. It was a way to envision our future, dancing together into the twilight of dementia.

≈

On a bright August afternoon two months before Dick died, we learned that another Oak Hill resident had passed away. He told me, "I'll stay through this next waltz."

Two days before his death, we danced together for the last time. Deep in the night, I sang to him and held his hands. When I crooned "Swing Low, Sweet Chariot," he began to move our arms in time to my song, swaying them from side to side. It was as if we were waltzing—he, supine, I, sitting next to him. Then I hummed "The Skaters' Waltz"—the tune I'd murmured as a child while ice-skating—and we continued our dance.

≈

The Dance of Death, or *Danse Macabre*, was depicted in the Middle Ages during the Black Death. Artists rendered the dance in drawings from that era. In them, people from every walk of life link hands in a solemn dance. A figure dressed as a skeleton leads them to the graveyard.

My husband and I had joined hands in our last waltz. Then Death summoned him and seized his hands.

≈

When I awoke early the next morning, the nurse and two aides were bathing him. Quietly, gently, they ministered to him. I opened my eyes to this sight. Looking up at the scene from my mattress on the floor, it seemed if they were angels, and this a sacrament.

That night, we'd danced our last waltz; by morning, he was in a liminal state, somewhere between the living and the dead. His body was rigid, his eyes and mouth open. He'd entered a coma. *Coma* comes from a Greek word meaning "deep sleep." Often, people will lapse into a coma before they die, a deep state of unconsciousness from which they can't be aroused. They can neither eat nor drink. They still hear what's said but can't respond. I'd look into Dick's eyes and smile. No response. I'd hold his cool hand and squeeze it. No response.

Then his fingers turned a deep purplish blue, like darkening skies before a summer storm. Beautiful, if one did not think about why they'd turned that color.

≈

After Dick fell into the coma, our friend Sylvia returned to sit by his bedside. She said, "Most of his spirit already has departed. It's there,"

IN THE EVENING, WE'LL DANCE

she gestured, her right arm raised and angled upward, toward the sky framed by the windows behind her.

I knew that Dick probably could hear me and assumed that he still could feel my touch. When a person is dying, hearing and touch are the last to go. The sense of smell is lost first, then taste, then sight.

Dick's eyes were wide open and unblinking during his remaining two days. They were glazed, no longer receiving nor emitting light—those eyes that often had been so luminous. If he could have spoken, Dick might have uttered the words of the psalmist: "My strength fails me; / and the light of my eyes, even that has gone from me." A friend said it was as if he were seeing beyond this world but was still of this world.

I asked the hospice doctor if this was typical. He said it was not. He said that most people die with their eyes fully closed; some die with their eyes partially open.

I didn't detect fear in Dick's eyes. The doctor reminded me that some people want to greet death "with their eyes wide open." Knowing my husband's inner strength and his awareness—despite the dementia—that his death was near, this seemed possible to me.

≈

In the middle of that night, I finally turned off the CD player, with its soothing piano melodies by Schumann, Fauré, and Brahms. I wanted only the sound of my voice, quietly talking or singing as I lay next to him.

I spoke of the night we met and fell in love. I spoke of his children, of the time we built our log home, of the year we lived in Spain, and of our other travels. I reminded him of the many gifts he'd given me during our years together, of his wonderful qualities, of what I loved about him.

Then I began to sing to comfort him. I couldn't bring myself to sing the tune he'd often sung to me in the last years of his life, "You Are My Sunshine." I knew I'd not make it through that song's plea: "Please don't take my sunshine away." It was night, winter was nigh, and my sunshine was going away.

Instead, I sang whatever came to mind: "Always," "All the Pretty Horses," "Silent Night," "Shenandoah," "Swing Low, Sweet Chariot," and "The Water Is Wide."

> *The water is wide; I cannot cross over,*
> *And neither have I wings to fly.*
> *Give me a boat that can carry two*
> *And both shall row - my love and I*
> *And both shall row - my love and I.*

≈

My friends may have understood what I was doing when I sang through the night, but I did not. I thought my singing was simply solace for my husband. That was true, but there was more to it. Days after his death, I read an old fairy tale, "The Emperor's Nightingale." And then I understood.

In the story, the emperor falls ill. He's "cold and pale," as was my husband. Death waits in the shadows. During the night, the emperor calls for music. Everyone in the court has fallen asleep, but suddenly the little nightingale appears at his window. She bargains with Death: If she sings through the night, will Death let the emperor live? Death is dismissive; the bird is far too small to sing all night long.

She breaks into song and sings until dawn. Death is defeated. The emperor awakes and thanks the nightingale: "I saw Death at my side last night, but you have sent him away."

Like the nightingale, I sang in hopes of keeping Death at bay.

Epilogue

Each night before bed, I go to the fireplace mantel, where the brass urn holding Dick's ashes stands. A lidded urn signifies oneness and the triumph over death in Chinese Buddhism. I don't know about the triumph over death, but I do seek a sense of oneness with my late husband. Usually, I press my forehead against the urn's cold, hard surface. Then I recreate him in my imagination. It's a physical sense of him I'm after. Sometimes I begin with his feet, sometimes with the top of his head. I work my way up or down his body. Sometimes I imagine his body clothed. Sometimes not. Once conjured, I breathe him in.

At first, I only could vivify the man who'd recently died: very thin, frail, and needy. To remember him as he was, before the dementia, was difficult. He was in one stage or another of the disease for more than a third of our forty-two years together. I gradually reclaimed memories of him when he was healthy: lean, strong, competent.

My interest was not in restoring him, an after-and-before that would return him to his original condition. I didn't want those images to replace my memories of Dick as he neared the end of his life. I wanted to retain both—the younger and the older, the vibrant man and the frail one. I wanted to hold them side by side.

≈

Although his speech was reduced to a whisper near the end, for most of his life Dick had a baritone voice that filled a room—not because it was loud but because it had a beautiful resonance. When something is resonant, it continues to sound in our ears. Or in our memories.

After Dick died, I chased after him, like a dog running in its sleep.

He was gone. Gone. I'd silently repeat his name, as if that would conjure him up: "DickCain/DickCain/DickCain." The sound of my heartbeat.

I immediately understood why the term "widowhood" is employed to describe a practice used in training homing pigeons. The author Susan Orlean tells us that pigeon trainers keep mating pairs apart "to increase their longing for each other" so they will hasten home. To ease my longing, I set about crafting a dwelling place built with words. In that way, I kept my husband alive.

≈

The act of writing an essay is described by the author Cynthia Ozick as "walking around a thought." The words of my husband were the thoughts around which I walked. Over the seventeen years of his dementia, Dick spoke or wrote the words that entitle my essays. They capture his voice as we lived through his decline.

I wrote the essays slowly, tentatively. I wrote them in no particular order, in fits and starts. At times, I stalled. Dick died. Then my mother. Then our dog, Phoenix. And after that? A pandemic. Millions died. "What's the point?" I wondered. Our story seemed insignificant amid so much death.

Sometimes, I had to walk away from the writing. If I dove into that sea of grief, I feared I would drown. I had to let time elapse in order to gauge the distance we'd travelled and to comprehend what I'd learned. Sometimes, I had to wait for the strength to revisit the losses, the crises, his death.

When I wrote, I waited for a swarm of ideas to coalesce, like a murmuration of roosting starlings that swoops and soars, shaping spirals, creatures, and clouds. I searched for words to give shape to my thoughts. I wanted to make meaning of it all.

≈

The essays were written about Dick, but they also were written to him. As such, they resemble a literary apostrophe, a passage in a poem or play in which the speaker addresses someone who isn't present. I addressed my late husband: *My love, this is what we lived through. This is how agonized and frightened and determined and loving we were. This is how valiant you were.*

As his life neared its end, Dick told me, "I love you the same as you love me. It keeps me moving." That love still keeps me moving.

≈

During the memorial service for Dick, I stood in the pulpit, braced myself, and faced the gathered family and friends. I quoted a passage from Joni Mitchell's "A Case of You." Commentators describe the song as "a gorgeously yearning ballad" that's filled with "raw emotion, vulnerability, and love." It suited our marriage, both in its intoxicating and enduring aspects. We drank one another in, like "holy wine," and yet stayed steady on our feet.

I recited Mitchell's lines at the memorial service. If I'd sung them, my voice would have soared like hers does on the word *you*—a long, upward trilling like a crazed birdsong. My husband was that kind of *you*.

≈

Shortly after his death, I had this dream: *Dick is cuddled next to me. I tell myself, "No, that can't be. I'm imagining it." Nonetheless, I continue to feel him close to me. I have the sensation of an embodied presence. I turn over to face his side of the bed. He's there! He's his handsome, brown-eyed self. He looks as he did when I first met him forty-two years ago. I kiss him.*

My dream transports us to a rustic house that resembles our log cabin. We sit facing one another at a table, like the old oak table that stood by the south-facing windows. We talk about ordinary, daily things. Not idly, but calmly.

Then we get up from our chairs and go to the door that opens to the yard and gardens. We look outside, but once we step over the threshold, he disappears. He's gone. I remain.

I don't feel sad or alarmed that he left me. Rather, I'm so pleased that he has been with me for that little while.

For Further Reading

Ballenger, Jesse F. *Self, Senility, and Alzheimer's Disease in Modern America: A History.* Johns Hopkins UP, 2006.

Basting, Anne Davis. *Forget Memory: Creating Better Lives for People with Dementia.* Johns Hopkins UP, 2009.

Bayley, John. *Elegy for Iris.* Picador, 1999.

Boss, Pauline. *Loving Someone Who Has Dementia: How to Find Hope While Coping with Stress and Grief.* Jossey-Bass, 2011.

Bryden, Christine. *Dancing with Dementia: My Story of Living Positively with Dementia.* Jessica Kingsley Publishers, 2005.

Conaway, James. "Absences: On Losing, by Degrees, One's Father." *Harper's*, June 1991, pp. 63-67.

Coutts, Marion. *The Iceberg: A Memoir.* Atlantic Books, 2014.

Doka, Kenneth J., editor. *The Longest Loss: Alzheimer's Disease and Dementia.* Hospice Foundation of America, 2015.

Fazio, Sam. *The Enduring Self in People with Alzheimer's: Getting to the Heart of Individualized Care.* Health Professions Press, 2008.

Gawande, Atul. *Being Mortal: Medicine and What Matters in the End.* Metropolitan Books, 2014.

Graff-Radford, Jonathon, and Angela M. Lunde. *Mayo Clinic on Alzheimer's Disease and other Dementias.* Mayo Clinic Press, 2020.

Groopman, Jerome. *The Anatomy of Hope: How People Prevail in the Face of Illness.* Random House, 2005.

Hampl, Patricia. *I Could Tell You Stories: Sojourns in the Land of Memory.* Norton, 1999.

Harper, Lynn Casteel. *On Vanishing: Mortality, Dementia, and What It Means to Disappear.* Catapult, 2020.

Hendershott, Anne. *The Reluctant Caregivers: Learning to Care for a Loved One with Alzheimer's.* Bergin & Garvey, 2000.

Hoblitzelle, Olivia Ames. *Ten Thousand Joys & Ten Thousand Sorrows: A Couple's Journey Through Alzheimer's*. Penguin Group, 2008.

Hoolihan, Patricia. *Hands and Heart Together: Daily Meditations for Caregivers*. Holy Cow! Press, 2021.

Hughes, Holly J., editor. *Beyond Forgetting: Poetry and Prose about Alzheimer's Disease*. Kent State UP, 2009.

Ignatieff, Michael. *Scar Tissue*. Farrar, Straus and Giroux, 1994.

Ingram, Jay. *The End of Memory: A Natural History of Aging and Alzheimer's*. Thomas Dunne Books, 2014.

Johnson, Caroline. *The Caregiver: Poems*. Holy Cow! Press, 2018.

Kitwood, Tom. *Dementia Reconsidered: The Person Comes First*. 1997. Open UP, 2001.

Kleinman, Arthur. *The Soul of Care: The Moral Education of a Husband and a Doctor*. Viking, 2019.

Kosik, Kenneth S., and Ellen Clegg. *The Alzheimer's Solution: How Today's Care Is Failing Millions and How We Can Do Better*. Prometheus, 2010.

Lock, Margaret. *The Alzheimer Conundrum: Entanglements of Dementia and Aging*. Princeton UP, 2013.

Mead, Rebecca. "The Sense of an Ending." *The New Yorker*, 20 May 2013, pp. 92-103.

Mortier, Erwin. *Stammered Songbook: A Mother's Book of Hours*. Translated by Paul Vincent. Pushkin Press, 2015.

Perlman, Jim, Deborah Cooper, Mara Hart, and Pamela Mittlefehldt. *Beloved on the Earth: 150 Poems of Grief and Gratitude*. Holy Cow! Press, 2009.

Post, Stephen G., and Jade C. Angelica. *Dignity for Deeply Forgetful People: How Caregivers Can Meet the Challenges of Alzheimer's Disease*. Johns Hopkins UP, 2022.

Power, G. Allen. *Dementia Beyond Disease: Enhancing Well-Being*. Health Professions Press, 2016.

Sabat, Steven R. *Alzheimer's Disease and Dementia: What Everyone Needs to Know*. Oxford UP, 2018.

——. *The Experience of Alzheimer's Disease: Life Through a Tangled Veil*. Wiley-Blackwell, 2001.

Sacks, Oliver. *Hallucinations*. Vintage, 2013.

——. "Music and Identity: Dementia and Music Therapy." *Musicophilia: Tales of Music and the Brain*. Vintage Books, 2008.

Santulli, Robert B., and Kesstan Blandin. *The Emotional Journey of the Alzheimer's Family*. Dartmouth College Press, 2015.

Shabahangi, Nader Robert, and Bogna Szymkiewicz. *Deeper into the Soul: Beyond Dementia and Alzheimer's Toward Forgetfulness Care*. Elders Academy Press, 2008.

Silverstone, Barbara, and Helen Kandel Hyman. *You and Your Aging Parent: A Family Guide to Emotional, Social, Health, and Financial Problems*. 4th ed., Oxford UP, 2008.

Simpson, Robert, and Anne Simpson. *Through the Wilderness of Alzheimer's: A Guide in Two Voices*. Augsburg Fortress Press, 1999.

Singh, Kathleen Dowling. *The Grace in Dying: A Message of Hope, Comfort, and Spiritual Transformation*. HarperOne, 2013.

Strohminger, Nina, and Shaun Nichols. "Your Brain, Your Disease, Your Self." *New York Times*, 21 Aug. 2014, p. SR10.

Swinton, John. *Dementia: Living in the Memories of God*. Eerdmans Publishing, 2012.

Taylor, Jill Bolte. *My Stroke of Insight: A Brain Scientist's Personal Journey*. Viking, 2006.

Thibault, Jane Marie, and Richard L. Morgan. *No Act of Love Is Ever Wasted: The Spirituality of Caring for Persons with Dementia*. Upper Room Books, 2009.

Webb, Gisela. "Intimations of the Great Unlearning." *Cross Currents*, vol. 51, no. 3, fall 2001, pp. 324-36.

Whitehouse, Peter J. *The Myth of Alzheimer's*. St. Martin's Griffin, 2008.

Acknowledgments

Many thanks to Jim Perlman, publisher of Holy Cow! Press, for his perceptive reading of and enthusiastic support for this book. I also want to recognize the designer, Anton Khodakovsky; John Connelly, who provided the beautiful cover photo; and Will Weaver, who suggested I contact Holy Cow! Press.

Endless gratitude to Elizabeth Blair, Patricia Weaver Francisco, Susan Hawkinson, and Teresa Alto for your careful, loving attention to many drafts of the manuscript, for sharing your insights, and for believing in this project. You have made this work better than it otherwise would have been. I also appreciate the responses to several essays provided by Jackie Solem, Loree Miltich, and Catherine Schroeder. My thanks to the people who kindly shared personal experiences that made their way into my essays: Yvonne Byrd, Joyce Peraaho, Gail Otteson, and John Ostroot.

I'm so grateful for the dear friends whose support sustained me over the years of writing and caregiving: Doug and Sylvia Olney, Susan Hawkinson, Stan Cronister, and "The Airheads" (Darlene Freeman, K.C. Neustrom, Loree Miltich, and Paulette Jerome). I give thanks to our dedicated respite caregivers, without whom I would not have been able to continue my teaching and writing. Thanks also to the family members and friends who offered words of encouragement about this project. You kept me going!

I am indebted to Dr. David Goodall, Dick's beloved physician; Dr. Maria Lapid, his wonderful geriatric psychiatrist at Mayo Clinic; and the staff at Oak Hill Assisted Living. I will never forget the attentive care you gave to Dick. You helped stabilize my husband during some tumultuous periods, which enabled me to press on with my writing.

I could not have continued to be a teacher, a caregiver, and a writer during several difficult years without the understanding and encouragement of my colleagues at Itasca Community College (ICC). To ICC's administrators, Dr. Barbara McDonald and Dr. Mike Johnson, my gratitude. Many thanks to librarian Steve Bean, who provided invaluable research assistance.

I want to recognize Michael Goldberg, host of "Stay Human Radio" on KAXE/KBXE-fm, for his championing of writers and storytellers in our region.

My gratitude to the Minnesota State Arts Board and the Arrowhead Regional Arts Council for grants which provided me with the time and resources to complete this work. I am fortunate to live in Minnesota, where the arts are supported.

So many people have sustained me over the years of Dick's dementia and the writing of this book. Please forgive me if I have inadvertently omitted your name.

And, always, to my family: my parents; my sister, Linda Stromgren; Jenny, Anna, and Joe Cain; and Ruth Cain. With gratitude and love for those who came before and those who support me now.

About the Author

ANNE-MARIE ERICKSON was born in the western Minnesota prairie town of Benson, the granddaughter of Norwegian immigrants. She attended Augsburg College in Minneapolis, where she earned a B.A. in American Studies. Following a move to northern Minnesota, she received an M.A. in English from Bemidji State University. For many years, she was a freelance writer. Her journalism, poetry, essays, and book reviews have appeared in regional publications; this is her first book. She taught English at Itasca Community College in Grand Rapids, Minnesota, and Mangold Institute, in Madrid, Spain. She has received support from the Minnesota State Arts Board, as well as the Arrowhead Regional Arts Council. She currently writes, reads, gardens, and enjoys the lakes, walking paths, music, and visual arts available in Grand Rapids. For more information, visit anne-marie-erickson-books.com.